your

A Guide to Assertive Living

Perfect Right

Robert E. Alberti, Ph.D.
Michael L. Emmons, Ph.D.

Impact Publishers
Post Office Box 1094
San Luis Obispo, California 93406

Editions

First Edition, October, 1970
Second Edition, January, 1974
Third Edition, May, 1978
Fourth Edition, April, 1982
Fifth Edition, July, 1986

Third Printing, February, 1987

Library of Congress Cataloging in Publication Data

Alberti, Robert E.
   Your perfect right.

   Bibliography: p.
   Includes index.
   1. Assertiveness (Psychology) 2. Interpersonal
communication. I. Emmons, Michael L. II. Title.
BF575.A85A43   1986   158'.1   86-7267
ISBN 0-915166-08-9
ISBN 0-915166-07-0 (pbk.)

Cover design by Sharon Schnare, San Luis Obispo, California

Printed in the United States of America

Published by **Impact ◈ Publishers**
POST OFFICE BOX 1094
SAN LUIS OBISPO, CALIFORNIA 93406

Contents

1 Assertiveness and You 1

2 What Is Your Perfect Right? 5

3 Your Personal Growth Log 17

4 What Does It Mean to Be "Assertive"? 25

5 Examples of Assertive, Non-assertive, and
    Aggressive Behavior 35

6 "I Couldn't Think of What to Say!" 43

7 Measuring Your Assertiveness 55

8 Goal For It! 63

9 Don't Let Your Thoughts Stop You! 73

10 There's Nothing to Be Afraid Of 85

11 Developing Assertive Behavior Skills 95

12 One Step At a Time 101

13 Assertiveness Builds Equal Relationships 109

14 Anger is Not a Four-Letter Word 125

15 Must We Put Up With Put Downs? 139

16 Assertiveness Works at Work, Too 145

17 Assertion and Sexuality 157

18 Helping Others Live With
    the New Assertive You 171

19 Beyond Assertiveness 179

Appendices 193

Bibliography 212

Index 214

Acknowledgements

Do you know anyone who claims to have written a book alone? Don't you believe it! Not every book has joint authors, of course, but every book is the product of the efforts of a number of people. It is never possible to thank them all enough.

Joseph Wolpe and the late Michael Serber stimulated and encouraged our early work with assertiveness training. Cyril Franks offered us review space in *Behavior Therapy* when only a handful of people had ever *heard* of "assertive training."

Carita and Charles Merker gave generously of their time and talents to help make possible the publication of the first edition.

Lachlan MacDonald edited the first two editions, and served for a time as agent and consultant for Impact Publishers.

Margaret Porter edited the fifth edition, helping us dump some excess baggage and lighten up the text.

The response of our students and readers has been a major influence in keeping us "honest," and in keeping the book up to date.

We had no idea in the summer of 1970 when we began this project that we would produce five editions, over half a million copies, and a successful publishing enterprise in the process. More important is the effect this book has had in the lives of hundreds of thousands of people. We are at once humbled and delighted with the results of our writing.

Our special appreciation goes to Deborah Alberti and Kay Emmons. Excellent models of assertiveness themselves, they have been endless sources of encouragement, love, and support. Both contributed their efforts from the beginning to help this project succeed. They made it all possible; without them there would have been no book. To them we rededicate this effort.

R.E.A.
M.L.E.

San Luis Obispo, California
March, 1986

Assertiveness and You

Be fair with others, but then keep after them until they're fair with you.

— Alan Alda

Joan was really upset when her neighbor came over and talked nonstop for forty-five minutes about neighborhood gossip. Mostly, she was upset with herself for letting it happen...again.

Frederick looked at his watch — 7:15. Laura would be furious, or worried sick, he knew. His boss had appeared at Frederick's desk at 4:55 and asked him to get this report ready for the Board meeting at 8:15 in the morning.

Travis and Linda were not sure if the waiter had forgotten them, was ignoring them, or was simply very busy. He had not been at their table for at least fifteen minutes. And they had theater tickets...

Anger, confusion, even a feeling of helplessness can result from situations like these. How can you communicate your feelings when such frustrations come up? There are no easy answers, but there are answers, if you are willing to make the effort.

Changing yourself is hard work, but you can do it. Millions of folks have learned to express themselves more effectively through the process called *assertiveness training*. You'll find in the chapters that follow a proven step-by-step procedure for improving your relationships with others. If you'll work at it, we are confident it can work for you.

The process itself is fairly simple. We'll give you some background information, some examples, and a series of specific procedures for you to follow. What you'll have to do — if you decide to try this approach — is read carefully and carry out the steps outlined.

We don't want to help you manipulate others. There is too much of that in the world already. Assertiveness is a tool for making your relationships more *equal* — for avoiding the one-down feeling that often comes when you fail to express what you really want.

Is this stuff mainly for those who aren't able to stand up for themselves? Partly. We wrote the first edition of this book for just such persons. We have learned a lot since 1970, however, and one thing we now know is that *everyone* needs a hand at times in getting along better with others.

How do you respond when...

...you want to cut short a telephone sales pitch?
...a co-worker puts you down?
...your spouse gives you a dirty look?
...a neighbor blasts his stereo until 3 a.m.?
...one of your children snaps at you?

In these and similar situations we all need some sort of "survival tactics" — some ways to respond which let others know something's wrong, while preserving the dignity of everyone involved. Some folks handle such situations by "swallowing" their feelings, saying nothing, and remaining upset. Others "blast" the offender in an effort to punish or regain the upper hand.

We are advocating *equality* as a style. Not "getting your way." Not "getting back at" the other person. And not "turning the other cheek." We think the important thing is your own feeling of self-worth.

You don't have to intimidate others in order to avoid being intimidated. And you don't have to allow yourself to be pushed around by anybody. By learning to be effectively assertive, you can deal with such upsets directly and honestly, and keep everyone on an equal footing — most of the time, anyway.

Many popular books talk about "assertiveness" as a technique for getting your way. That is not our goal. You won't find gimmicks on how to manipulate others in this book. Instead, we'll help you to clarify your personal goals in relationships, and we'll show you how to retain a sense of control over your own life without trying to control others in the process.

In later chapters, the concepts of *aggressive*, *assertive* and *nonassertive* behavior are illustrated with lots of examples and specific instructions — minus the usual psychological jargon. In a separate professional edition of this book, we have expanded upon the theoretical and procedural aspects of developing assertive behavior, as a guide for professionals who are engaged in facilitating personal growth in their clients.

Whether your goals are personal, social, job-related, or world-changing, you will find a careful reading-and-practice approach to these ideas and procedures will help you to develop more effective self-expression and healthier relationships.

Before you go on to the next chapter, think a bit about your own goals. Why did you pick up this book? Are you looking for help in specific areas of your life — on the job perhaps, or with your family relationships? In what ways would you like your life to be different? Chapter 8 goes into specifics about setting goals for your growth, but give a few moments thought now to what you'd like to gain from reading *Your Perfect Right*. Then, when you're ready, push ahead and let's find out what this "assertiveness" stuff is all about.

What Is Your Perfect Right?

*Between people, as among nations, respect of each
other's rights insures the peace.*

— Benito Juarez

Do you ever feel helpless, powerless, ineffective? Do you
sometimes get pushy in an effort to make yourself heard?

Is it difficult for you to make your wishes known to
others? Do you often find yourself "low person on the totem
pole"? Are you sometimes pushed around by others because
of your own inability to stand up for yourself? Or do you push
others around in order to get your way?

The Assertive Alternative

Assertiveness is an alternative to personal powerlessness
and manipulation. You will find in this book a program which
develops self-confidence *and* respect for others. We firmly
believe in the equal value of every human being. This book
celebrates that belief, and encourages positive relationships
between and among persons who respect and value each
other.

Over the past two decades, some progress has been
made in the United States toward the development of a
society based upon these values. Individuals have spoken out
much more clearly, and some intolerable conditions have

changed. Relationships, from the most intimate of love partners to the most distant of neighbors and co-workers, have begun to reflect a more equal valuing of both persons. Assertiveness training has had something to do with some of those needed changes. This book, first published in 1970, has been a contributor to that process.

Popular ideas about what it means to be assertive cover an amazing range. A recent "Ziggy" cartoon illustrates the unfortunate image many hold. The single-frame sketch shows our hero approaching a door labeled "Assertiveness Training Class." Below that sign is another message on the door: "Don't Bother to Knock, Barge Right In!" We have tried to foster a less aggressive view of self-expression, and to correct that pushy notion of assertiveness.

Barriers to Self-Expression

In helping thousands of persons learn to value themselves and to express themselves directly and honestly, we have found three particularly difficult barriers to self-assertion:

- Many people do not believe that they have the *right* to be assertive;
- Many people are highly *anxious* or *fearful* about being assertive;
- Many people lack the *skills* for effective self-expression.

In this book we've addressed these barriers to personal power and healthy relationships. You'll find here proven, effective tools to overcome them.

Assertiveness and Personal Power

This is not a proposal for political, economic, or social revolution. We are concerned with power on a much more personal level — at home, on the job, at school, in stores and restaurants, in club meetings, wherever the sense of personal insignificance or frustration is encountered. Yet we also hope to empower persons to help build a society which is responsive to human needs.

You know the ways your power is diminished every day. Some are trivial, some important. Has anyone ever cut in front of you in a line? Do you have difficulty saying "no" to persuasive people? Are you able to express warm, positive feelings to someone? Can you comfortably begin a conversation with strangers at a party? Have you ever regretted "stepping on" someone else in trying to gain your own objectives?.

Many people find situations like these uncomfortable or irritating, and are at a loss for just the right action. There is no one "right way" to handle such events, but there are some basic principles which will help you to gain confidence and effectiveness in your relationships with others.

Here's a working definition:

Assertive behavior promotes equality in human relationships, enabling us to act in our own best interests, to stand up for ourselves without undue anxiety, to express honest feelings comfortably, to exercise personal rights without denying the rights of others.

The person who typically behaves non-assertively is likely to think of an appropriate response after the opportunity has passed. An aggressive response, on the other hand, is too strong, and may make a deep and negative impression for which one may later be sorry. By developing a more adequate repertoire of assertive behavior, you may choose appropriate and self-fulfilling responses in a variety of situations.

Assertiveness Is Positive and Healthy

Learning to make assertive responses will reduce the anxiety you may feel in dealing with others. Research has shown that, by developing the ability to stand up for yourself and do things on your own initiative, you can cut down your

stress and increase your sense of worth as a person —
whether your present style is nonassertive or aggressive.

Do you go through life inhibited, giving in to the wishes
of others, holding your own desires inside yourself — or
conversely, pushing others around in order to have your way?
Even such physical complaints as headaches, general fatigue,
stomach disturbances, rashes, and asthma may be related to a
failure to develop assertive behavior. Assertiveness can help
you avoid such symptoms. You can be healthier, more in
charge of yourself in relationships, more confident and
capable, more spontaneous in expressing your feelings. And
you'll likely find yourself more admired by others as well.

Aggression and assertion are commonly confused, but
assertive behavior does not push others around, deny their
rights, or run roughshod over people. Assertiveness reflects
genuine concern for *everybody's* rights.

Your Perfect Human Rights

Every individual is equal and has the same fundamental
human rights as others in a relationship, regardless of roles
and titles. We hope you'll learn to exercise *your* perfect rights
without infringing upon the rights of others. The *Universal
Declaration of Human Rights*, adopted by the United Nations
General Assembly in 1948, is an excellent statement of goals
for human relationships. We urge you to read through the
Declaration (see Appendix B), and let its principles encourage
you to support the rights of the individual — including
yourself!

Such a broad view of individual human rights can help
us, as citizens of a planet which is really very small, to
counteract the forces which pit us against one another in the
conflict of nations. We are all human beings after all,
dependent upon each other in many ways, and in need of
mutual support and understanding for our survival. Truly,
''we are the world.''

Unfortunately, society often evaluates human beings on

scales which rank some people better than others. Consider
these popular but false ideas:

adults are better than children
bosses are better than employees
men are better than women
whites are better than blacks
physicians are better than plumbers
teachers are better than students
politicians are better than voters
generals are better than privates
winners are better than losers
Americans are better than "foreigners"

and on and on. Our society's organizations tend to perpetuate
these myths, and to allow individuals in these roles to be
treated as if they were of lesser value as human beings. The
good news, however, is that lots of folks are finding ways to
express themselves.

Women Are Talking Back!

Particularly in the past decade, women have found their
voices once again, and have achieved long overdue gains in
recognition of their individual rights. The widespread offering
of assertiveness training for women, including a tremendous
number of specialized workshops in management and other
fields, is one hopeful sign. Women of all social viewpoints,
ethnic and socio-economic backgrounds, educational and
professional involvements — homemakers, hard hats, and
high ranking executives — have made phenomenal gains in
assertive expression.

Society has begun to recognize the inadequacy of an
"ideal" which identifies women as characteristically
"passive, sweet, submissive, accepting, warm, loving,
nurturing, empathetic." At long last, the assertive woman is
valued.

In their excellent book *The Assertive Woman* (which is
good reading for men, too), Stanlee Phelps and Nancy Austin

present the behavioral styles of four "women we all know."
Their characterizations of *Doris Doormat, Agatha Aggressive,
Iris Indirect,* and *April Assertive* are self-explanatory by the
names alone. Yet, in describing the patterns of each, Phelps
and Austin help us to gain a clearer picture of the social mores
which have devalued assertiveness in women, Agatha gets
her way, though she hasn't many friends. Iris, the sly one,
also gains most of what she wants, and sometimes her
"victims" never even know it. Doris, although denied her
own wishes much of the time, is highly praised by men and by
the power structure as "a good woman." April's honesty and
forthrightness have often led her into trouble (at least until
recently) at home, at school, on the job, and even with other
women.

A degree of balance is now emerging. Women are
people, have rights, deserve equal recognition/status/pay,
are not inherently weaker, do not (except when they freely so
choose) belong in the home. Thus the assertive woman —
slowly and with considerable effort — is becoming a person
valued by society, by men, by other women. She is capable of
choosing her own lifestyle, free of dictates of tradition,
government, husband, children, social groups, bosses. She
may elect to be a homemaker and not fear intimidation by her
"liberated" sisters. She may elect to pursue a
male-dominated profession and enjoy confidence in her rights
and abilities.

In her sexual relationships, she can be comfortable
taking initiative, asking for what she wants (and thereby
freeing her partner from the expected role of making the first
move). She and her partner can share equally in the
expression of intimacy.

She can say "no" with firmness — and can make it stick.

As a consumer, she can make the marketplace respond to
her needs by refusing to accept shoddy merchandise, service,
or marketing techniques.

In short, the assertive *woman* is an assertive *person* who exhibits the qualities we espouse throughout this book; and she likes herself — and is liked — better for it!

Men Can Be Assertive Too!

Imagine the following scene: John's day has been exhausting; he has washed windows, mopped floors, completed three loads of wash, and continuously picked up and cleaned up after the children. He is now working hurriedly in the kitchen preparing for dinner. The children are running in and out of the house banging the door, screaming, throwing toys.

In the midst of this chaos, Mary arrives home from an equally trying day at her office. She offers a cursory "I'm home!" as she passes the kitchen on her way to the family room. Dropping her briefcase and kicking off her shoes, she flops in her favorite chair in front of the television set, calling out, "John, bring me a beer! I've had a helluva day!"

This scene is humorous partly because it seems highly unusual. After all, shouldn't *John* be the breadwinner, working at an office rather than at home? Isn't a *man's* place to go out and conquer the world on behalf of his family? To demonstrate his manhood, his macho, his strength and courage?

Unfortunately, we have for too long accepted as proper the stereotype of the male as "mighty hunter," who must protect and provide for his family. Indeed, from earliest childhood, the accepted male roles have encouraged assertive and often aggressive behavior in pursuit of this "ideal." Competitiveness, achievement, striving to be the best have been integral components of male child-rearing and formal schooling — much more so than for their sisters. Men have been treated as if they were by nature strong, active, decisive, dominant, cool, rational.

A growing number of men are acknowledging a great gap in their preparation for interpersonal relationships. Limited to only two options: the powerful, dominating aggressor or the

"97-pound weakling" with sand in his face, most have found neither to be particularly satisfying. Assertiveness has offered them an effective alternative.

Many men have begun to reject the aggressive, climbing, "success" stereotype in favor of a more balanced role and lifestyle. Psychological concepts of "masculinity" have changed to acknowledge the caring, nurturing side of men as well. And perhaps most significantly, men have recognized that they can accomplish their own life goals in assertive — not aggressive — ways. Professional advancement in all but the most stubbornly competitive fields is available for the competent, confident, assertive man.

Similarly, the assertive man is held in greater esteem in personal relationships. Family and friends are closer and have greater respect for the man who is comfortable enough with himself that he needn't put others down in order to put himself up. The honesty of assertiveness is an incalculable asset in close personal relationships, and assertive men are coming to value such closeness right along with the traditional rewards of economic success.

Gail Sheehy, in her 1976 book *Passages*, noted that many men who have lived the aggressive style in their 20s and 30s find that those achievements mean little in their later years. The values of personal intimacy, family closeness, and trusted friendships — all fostered by assertiveness, openness, honesty — are the lasting and important ones. The assertive man is finding himself too!

Society Often Discourages Assertiveness

Despite important gains, society's rewards for appropriate assertive behavior are still limited. The assertions of each individual, the right of self-expression without fear or guilt, the right to a dissenting opinion, and the unique contribution of each person — all need greater recognition. We must emphasize the difference between such appropriate assertion and the destructive aggression with which it is often confused.

The worlds of family, school, work, and church all have made it difficult to act assertively. Assertion is often actively discouraged, in subtle — or not so subtle — ways.

In the family, the child who decides to speak up for his or her rights is often promptly censored: "Don't you dare talk to your mother (father) that way!" "Children are to be seen, not heard." "Never let me hear you talk like that again!" Obviously, these common parental commands are not conducive to a child's assertion of self!

Teachers are frequently inhibitors of assertion. Quiet, well-behaved children who do not question authority are rewarded, whereas those who "buck the system" in some way are dealt with sternly. Educators acknowledge that the child's natural spontaneity in learning is conditioned out no later than the fourth or fifth grade, replaced by conformity to the school's approach.

The results of such upbringing effect functioning on the job, and the workplace itself often is no help. At work, employees are aware that typically one must not do or say anything that will rock the boat. The boss is in charge, and others feel obliged to go along with what is expected of them even if they consider the expectations completely inappropriate. Early work experiences often teach that those who speak up are not likely to obtain raises or recognition, and may even lose their jobs. You quickly learn to be a company person, to keep things running smoothly, to have few ideas of your own, to be careful how you act lest it get back to the boss. The lesson is clear again: be nonassertive in your work!

The teachings of many churches suggest that assertive behavior is somehow at odds with religious commitment. Such qualities as humility, self-denial, and self-sacrifice may be encouraged, to the exclusion of standing up for oneself. There is a mistaken notion that religious ideals must, in some mystical way, be incompatible with feeling good about oneself and with being calm and confident in relationships with others. Quite the contrary; assertiveness is not only compatible with the teachings of major religions, it frees you of self-defeating behavior, allowing you to be of greater service to others as well as to yourself!

Political institutions are not so likely as the home, school and church to influence early development of assertive behavior, but they do little to encourage its expression. Political decision-making remains largely inaccessible to the average citizen. Nevertheless, it is still true that the "squeaking wheel gets greased," and when individuals *do* become expressive enough, governments usually respond.

It is our hope that more adequately assertive expression will preclude the necessity of aggression among the activist politically alienated. The growth and successes of assertive citizen lobbies — the civil rights movement, Common Cause, the Grey Panthers, the various tax reform movements — are powerful evidence: assertion does work! And there may be no more important arena for its application than overcoming the sense of "What's the use? I can't make a difference." that tends to pervade the realm of personal political action.

We contend that *each of us has the right to be and to express ourselves, and to feel good [not powerless or guilty] about doing so, as long as we do not hurt others in the process.*

The institutions of society have so carefully taught us not to express even reasonable rights, that we may feel powerless to express ourselves, or guilty if we do stand up to be counted.

It's time for families, schools, businesses, churches, and governments to encourage individual self-assertion, and to stop limiting self-fulfilling actions.

Who Will Read This Book?

This book is written for all who wish to develop more enhancing lives for themselves. Hundreds of thousands of individuals who were unable to be adequately assertive have achieved greater self-fulfillment by following this assertiveness training program. We believe you can find similar help here. We are especially pleased that thousands of therapists have recommended the book as helpful reading for their clients.

Make the most of what we offer here to help yourself, and let us hear from you. Reader feedback and reports of others' work with assertiveness training have helped us to refine and update this work through five editions. With your help we can continue to make it even better!

3

Your Personal Growth Log

*Where I was born and where and how I have
lived is unimportant. It is what I have done with
where I have been that should be of interest.*
— Georgia O'Keeffe

We'd like to encourage you to get started now on your
own process of growth toward effective self-expression. A
simple way to do that is by starting a "personal growth log."
Nothing fancy, just a simple device for jotting notes about
how things are going in your life as you take this journey
toward greater assertiveness.

As a nautical device, a log is used as a daily record of a
ship's speed and progress. Much the same could be said for
the components of a personal growth log! Although we are not
really concerned with the speed of your change, we are
definitely interested in your progress. A daily record of your
assertiveness will help you judge your progress over time
and, after a few weeks, you'll find it provides a wealth of
information about your ongoing assertiveness.

Your log entries can include self-examination, notes on
your reading, goals, ... anything you'd like to keep track of.
Give at least some space to systematic observation of four
dimensions of your life which relate to assertiveness:
situations/persons, attitudes, behaviors, and *obstacles.*

We urge you to obtain a special notebook, pad, folder, whatever, so you can record your thoughts, observations, feelings, and progress.

A sample page of your log might look like this:

ASSERTIVENESS LOG FOR   **19**

Situations / Persons

Attitudes

Behaviors

Obstacles

Notes: Progress / Problems / Comments

If you'll keep it up regularly, your log can become a very important tool for your growth program — both to record your progress and to serve as a "motivator" to continue working on your personal development.

As you undertake specific changes in your life, you may wish to become more thorough in your log-keeping. The ideas which follow may be of some help.

Refer to the Assertiveness Inventory (Chapter 7), and determine those *situations* and *persons* which you can handle effectively and those which are troublesome. Write down the results in your log. Pay particular attention to any patterns which may appear. Are you more adequate with strangers than with intimates, for example, or perhaps vice versa? Can you readily stand up for your rights, but fall down on expressing affection? Do such factors as age, sex, or roles of the other person make a difference?

It is very difficult to accurately measure *attitudes*, and particularly difficult to be objective about one's own. Nevertheless, we encourage you to write down in your log your feelings about your right to behave assertively. Look at the various situations and people in the definition of assertive behavior (Chapter 2), and in the situations described in the Assertiveness Inventory (Chapter 7). Do you feel, for example, that it's okay to respond when you've been criticized by someone in authority?

Evaluating your *behavior* in a given situation is not as difficult, but may take longer. In Chapter 6, we'll describe in detail several components of behavior which are key to any assertive act. If you monitor your own behavior carefully for a time (a week or more is a good idea), and record your observations regularly in your log, you will have a good idea of your own effectiveness with eye contact, facial expression, body posture, and the other components noted there. It will probably help if you make it a point to watch some other people you consider effectively assertive, and to note in your log some of their behavioral qualities as well.

Obstacles may be the easiest area for you to keep track of. We know that most people want to act assertively. However, for many, there are barriers which seem to make assertion difficult.

Common obstacles within you include *anxiety* (Fear of the possible consequences: Maybe the other person won't like me, or will hit me, or will think I'm crazy. Or maybe I'll make a fool of myself. Or maybe I'll fail to get what I want. Or maybe I can't put my finger on it, but I just feel anxious!), and *lack of skills* (I don't know how to meet girls. What do I do to express a political opinion? I never learned how to show affection.).

Perhaps the most difficult external obstacles are the *other people in your life* (Parents, friends, lovers, roommates, and others have an interest in making it difficult for you to change, even if they believe they want you to be more assertive).

Record in your log those obstacles which you think are making assertiveness more difficult for you.

If you will take the time and effort to keep a log and, as you learn more about assertiveness, to proceed carefully and thoroughly with your self-assessment, you will find that the results will help to pinpoint specifically what you will need to do to increase your assertiveness. At every point, of course, you may choose whether to carry this personal growth program further, and what direction you will take. And *choice* is the key element in your assertiveness anyway!

Every week or so, carefully examine your log entries: situations, attitudes, behaviors, obstacles, notes. Look for patterns. Remember to evaluate your strengths as well as your weaknesses.

The first week or two of entries in your log should give you a good picture of how you are doing now, and provide a basis for setting goals for yourself. While we have not yet presented a systematic process for setting goals (that comes in Chapter 8), we encourage you to continue to think about your own hopes for improved assertiveness, and to make notes in your log about them.

Your observations of yourself, as recorded in your log, might indicate that you have difficulty with people in authority — that you do not believe you have a right to speak up to them, that you cannot maintain good eye contact with them, and that you are very anxious around such people. Each of these items is something you can work on individually and overcome through the process of assertiveness training described in this book.

Changing long-standing behaviors, aggressive, nonassertive, or others, is difficult. Your log can be a crucial asset in the process of change. As you become aware of your behavior patterns, you can begin to choose deliberately, and act in ways which will move you toward your goals. As your initial awkward attempts at assertion are rewarded — "Hey, it worked!" — you'll find the assertive choice will become easier and easier.

Start your log today with notes about your reading thus far in the book. Keep using your log throughout your reading of *Your Perfect Right* and beyond, to keep a careful record of how you're doing as you apply these concepts in your own life. Your log will provide a series of "bench marks" so you can watch yourself grow. It will help motivate you to work at your progress. It will remind you how far you really have come — especially valuable at those times when you begin to think you aren't getting anywhere! Reading your log will reassure you that you are making progress, even if it is slow.

Your log will help you to be more systematic about your work on assertiveness. And that can make all the difference!

As you begin keeping a regular record of your behavior and interactions with others, you will learn some new things about yourself. If you find complex and severe shortcomings in any of the behavioral areas we've discussed, it is possible that you will want professional assistance in reaching your goal. Particularly if you experience very high levels of anxiety about being assertive, we suggest contact with a qualified counselor, psychologist, psychiatrist, or other therapist. Your local community mental health center or college/university counseling center can assist you in finding someone to help. Also, Appendix C identifies standards which may help you to select a professional therapist.

HOW ARE YOU DOING?

From time to time throughout *Your Perfect Right,* we've inserted this "break" in the text to get you to pause and take stock. No big formal deal — just a periodic checkup to help you stay on track.

Take some time now to answer the questions below. Be honest with yourself, and let the answers guide your next steps.

• Have you read and understood all the material in the previous chapters?
• Do our explanations and examples fit with your own experience?
    If not, can you adapt them to your needs?
• Are you doing the exercises and answering the questions we have raised?
• Has "assertiveness" begun to mean something real to you?
• Have you set some preliminary goals for your growth in assertiveness?
• Are you keeping a log of your progress?
• Have you asked for help if you need it for anxiety or other obstacles?
• Have you identified your own shortcomings in assertiveness: anxiety, attitudes, social skills?

4

What Does It Mean to Be "Assertive"?

We are all controlled by the world in which we live.... The question is this: are we to be controlled by accidents, by tyrants, or by ourselves?

— B. F. Skinner

Assertiveness, as you have seen, is not a simple characteristic. The fact is, there is no general agreement on a definition of the term. Some suggest that the concept is so complex and has such diverse meaning as to be indefinable! Despite these complexities, we know from the experience of thousands of people that training in assertiveness can be valuable, if training procedures are carefully matched to individual needs.

In this chapter, we will examine several approaches to the concept of assertiveness. Our brief definition in Chapter 2 offers a starting point:

Assertive behavior promotes equality in human relationships, enabling us to act in our own best interests, to stand up for ourselves without undue anxiety, to express feelings honestly and comfortably, to exercise personal rights without denying the rights of others.

Let's examine those elements in greater detail: *To promote equality in human relationships* means to put both parties on an equal footing, to restore the balance of power by giving personal power to the ''underdog,'' to make it possible for everyone to gain and no one to lose.

To act in your own best interests refers to the ability to make your own decisions about career, relationships, life style and time schedule, to take initiative starting conversations and organizing activities, to trust your own judgment, to set goals and work to achieve them, to ask help from others, to participate socially.

To stand up for yourself includes such behaviors as saying no, setting limits on time and energy, responding to criticism or put-downs or anger, expressing or supporting or defending an opinion.

To express feelings honestly and comfortably means the ability to disagree, to show anger, to show affection or friendship, to admit fear or anxiety, to express agreement or support, to be spontaneous — all without painful anxiety.

To exercise personal rights relates to competency as a citizen, as a consumer, as a member of an organization or school or work group, as a participant in public events to express opinions, to work for change, to respond to violations of one's own rights or those of others.

To not deny the rights of others is to accomplish the above personal expressions without unfair criticism of others, without hurtful behavior toward others, without name-calling, without intimidation, without manipulation, without controlling others.

Thus, assertive behavior is a positive self-affirmation which also values the other people in your life. It contributes both to your personal life satisfaction and to the quality of your relationships with others.

Studies show that, as a direct result of gains in self-expressiveness, individuals have improved their self-esteem, reduced their anxiety, overcome depression, gained greater respect from others, accomplished more in terms of their life goals, increased their level of self-understanding, and improved their capacity to communicate more effectively with others. We can't promise those results for you, of course, but the evidence is impressive!

Assertive, Nonassertive, and Aggressive Behavior

The way we live in the late twentieth century presents some mixed messages about appropriate behavior. A typical example is found in common attitudes and teachings about human sexuality. While restraint is the sexual norm of the middle-class family, school and church, the popular media bombard audiences with a different view.

Aggressiveness is highly valued in male sexual behavior: the "lover" is glorified in print, on the screen, and by his peers. Paradoxically, he is cautioned to date "respectable" girls, and warned that sexual intercourse is allowable only after marriage. Women are given similar mixed messages. On one hand, they are expected to be sweet and innocently non-assertive; whereas on the other other they are rewarded for being sultry, seductive, and sensual.

Examples of such conflicts between *recommended* and *rewarded* behavior are evident in many other areas of life. Even though it is typically understood that one should respect the rights of others, all too often we observe that parents, teachers, business and government contradict these values in their own actions. Tact, diplomacy, politeness, refined manners, modesty, and self-denial are generally praised; yet to get ahead it is often acceptable to "step on" others.

The male child is carefully coached to be strong, brave,

and dominant. His aggressiveness is condoned and accepted — as in the pride felt by a father whose son gets in trouble for socking the neighborhood bully in the nose. Ironically, and a source of much confusion for the child, the same father will likely encourage his son to "have respect for his elders," "let others go first," and "be polite."

The athlete who participates in competitive sports is encouraged to be aggressive, perhaps even to bend the rules a little. That's O.K., because "It's not important how you play the game; it's just important that you win." Contrast the rewards for winning coaches with those for losing coaches who "build character." Woody Hayes, much-acclaimed former head football coach at Ohio State University, is quoted as saying, "Show me a good loser, and I'll show you a loser."

We believe that you should be able to *choose for yourself* how to act in a given circumstance. If your "polite restraint" response is too strong, you may be unable to make the choice to act as you would like. If your aggressive response is overdeveloped, you may be unable to achieve goals without hurting others. Freedom of choice and self-control are made possible by developing assertive responses for situations in which you have previously responded nonassertively or aggressively.

Contrasting assertive with nonassertive and aggressive actions will help to clarify these concepts. The chart displays several feelings and consequences typical for the person (sender) whose actions are nonassertive, assertive, or aggressive. Also shown, for each of these actions, are the likely consequences for the person toward whom the action is directed (receiver).

Non-Assertive Behavior	Aggressive Behavior	Assertive Behavior
As Sender	**As Sender**	**As Sender**
Self-denying	Self-enhancing at expense of another	Self-enhancing
Inhibited		Expressive
Hurt, anxious	Expressive	Feels good about self
Allows others to choose	Chooses for others	Chooses for self
Does not achieve desired goal	Achieves desired goal by hurting others	May achieve desired goal
As Receiver	**As Receiver**	**As Receiver**
Guilty or angry	Self-denying	Self-enhancing
Depreciates sender	Hurt, defensive humiliated	Expressive
Achieves desired goal at sender's expense	Does not achieve desired goal	May achieve desired goal

As the chart shows, a *nonassertive* response means that the sender is typically denying self-expression, and is inhibited from letting feelings show. People who behave nonassertively often feel hurt and anxious since they allow others to choose for them. They seldom achieve their own desired goals.

The person who carries a desire for self-expression to the extreme of *aggressive* behavior accomplishes goals at the expense of others. Although frequently self-enhancing and expressive of feelings in the situation, aggressive behavior

hurts other people in the process by making choices for them
and by minimizing their worth.

Aggressive behavior commonly results in a *putdown* of
the receiver. Rights denied, the receiver feels hurt, defensive,
and humiliated. His or her goals in the situation, of course,
are not achieved. Aggressive behavior may achieve the
sender's goals, but may also generate bitterness and
frustration which may later return as vengeance.

A number of professionals who work with assertiveness
training prefer to add a fourth category — *indirect aggression*
— to this model. They note that much aggressive behavior
takes the form of passive, non-confrontive action. Sometimes
such actions are sneaky or sly, other times they may simply be
double entendre. Characteristic of this style is the smiling,
friendly, agreeable behavior which hides a back-stabbing or
undermining action. We consider this category to be a form of
aggression, and have simplified our model by not dealing with
it separately. We do acknowledge its importance, however,
and will have more to say about it in Chapter 17.

Appropriately *assertive* behavior in the same situation
would be self-enhancing for the sender, an honest expression
of feelings, and will usually achieve the goal. When you
choose for yourself how to act, a good feeling typically (not
always) accompanies the assertive response, even when your
goals are not achieved.

Similarly, when the consequences of these three
contrasting behaviors are viewed from the perspective of the
the person receiving the action, a parallel pattern emerges.
Nonassertive behavior often produces feelings ranging from
sympathy to confusion to outright contempt for the sender.
Also, the receiver may feel guilt or anger at having achieved
goals at the sender's expense. The receiver of aggressive
actions is often hurt, defensive, put-down, or perhaps
aggressive in return. In contrast, assertion enhances the
feeling of self-worth of both parties, and permits both full
self-expression and achievement of goals.

In summary, then, it is clear that the sender is hurt by self-denial in nonassertive behavior; the receiver (or even both parties) may be hurt by aggressive behavior. In the case of assertion, neither person is hurt, and it is likely that both will succeed.

It is important to note that assertive behavior is *person-and-situation-specific,* not universal. That is, what may be considered assertive depends upon the persons involved and the circumstances of the situation. Although we believe the definitions and examples presented in this book are realistic and appropriate for most people and circumstances, individual differences must be considered. Cultural or ethnic background for example, may create an entirely different set of personal circumstances which would change the nature of "appropriateness" in assertive behavior.

Cultural Differences in Self-Assertion

While the desire for self-expression may be a basic human need, assertive behavior in interpersonal relationships is primarily characteristic of western cultures (although by no means limited to the U.S.A.).

In Oriental cultures, for example, "face" is extremely important. How one is seen by others is more important to an individual than is self-concept. The idea of assertiveness — in the Western sense of self-expression — is almost inappropriate for members of most Asian cultures.

Latin and Hispanic societies have emphasized the notion of "machismo" to the point that assertiveness — as we have defined it — seems rather tame, especially for men. In those cultures, a greater display of strength is the norm for self-expression.

Yet, people from those cultures where self-assertion traditionally has not been valued may be just those who most need its benefits. We are really very assertive in North America, by and large. People of other lands have tended to express themselves in ways we might consider non-assertive or aggressive. While for some cultures those styles represent thousands of years of tradition, it may be that current and future international relations require more open and direct communication, and a greater sense of equality — expressed on both sides of the table.

Classifying Behavior: "A Rose, By Any Other Name..."

"I told my father-in-law not to smoke his cigar in my house! Was that assertive or aggressive?"

Members of assertiveness training groups and workshops often ask trainers to classify a particular act as "assertive" or "aggressive." What criteria do make the important difference?

We have suggested that assertive and aggressive behavior differ principally in that the latter involves hurting, manipulating, or denying others in the course of expressing oneself.

Practitioners and writers with a psychoanalytic orientation have proposed that *intent* must be considered. That is, if you intended to hurt your father-in-law, that's aggressive; if you simply wanted to inform him of your wishes, you were acting assertively.

Many psychologists insist that behavior must be measurable according to its *effects*. Thus, if your father gets the assertive message and responds accordingly — by agreeing not to smoke — your behavior may be classified as assertive. If he pouts in a corner, or shouts, "Who do think you are?" your statement may have been aggressive, as described by this criterion.

Finally, as we have noted, the *social-cultural context* must be taken into account in classifying behavior as assertive or aggressive or nonassertive. A culture, for example, which regards honoring one's elders as one of its ultimate values may view the request as clearly out of line and aggressive, regardless of the behavior, response, or intent.

There are no absolutes in this area, and some criteria may be in conflict. A particular act may be at once assertive in *behavior* and *intent* (you wanted to and did express your feelings), aggressive in *response* (the other person could not handle your assertion), and nonassertive in the social *context* (your culture expects a powerful, put-down style). It's not always easy to classify human behavior!

A specific situation may vary considerably from the examples we discuss here. In any event, the question "Is it assertive or aggressive?" is not one which may be answered simply! Each situation ultimately must be evaluated on its own. The labels "nonassertive," "assertive," and "aggressive" themselves carry no magic, but they may be useful in assessing the appropriateness of a particular action.

Our concern is not with the labels, but with helping you to choose for yourself how you will act, and with helping you know that you have the tools you need to succeed.

Social Consequences of Assertion

While it is our purpose in *Your Perfect Right* to teach you skills so that you may improve your own ability to express yourself appropriately and responsibly, we believe strongly that self-expression must be modulated by its context. Just as freedom of speech does not convey the right to yell "fire" in a crowded theater, so the form of self-expression we advocate is one which considers its consequences.

The perfect right you have to say "no" exists alongside the other person's right to say "yes." And your desire to accomplish your goals through self-assertion must be weighed against the needs of the larger society. Speak out or write about any idea you choose to support, but recognize the other person's right to do the same. And be prepared to pay some dues — perhaps in jail — if your expression goes beyond words and includes civil disobedience. Just as there are taxes for those who accumulate wealth, there is a price to pay for freedom of expression.

While you have a perfect right to advocate a viewpoint, everyone else has the same right — and your views may conflict. Keep this in mind on your journey toward greater personal assertiveness.

Ten Key Points About Assertive Behavior

To summarize this chapter, here is a list of the key elements of assertive behavior:

1. Self-expressive;
2. Respectful of the rights of others;
3. Honest;
4. Direct and firm;
5. Equalizing, benefitting both self and relationship;
6. Verbal, including the content of the message (feelings, rights, facts, opinions, requests, limits);
7. Nonverbal, including the style of the message (eye contact, voice, posture, facial expression, gestures, distance, timing, fluency, listening);
8. Appropriate for the person and the situation, not universal;
9. Socially responsible;
10. Learned, not inborn.

Now you have a better idea of what it means to be assertive, and you are probably ready to begin taking steps toward increasing your own assertiveness.

The following chapter provides many examples of life situations calling for assertive action. It's likely you'll find yourself nodding in recognition as you read some of these!

5

Examples of Assertive, Non-assertive, and Aggressive Behavior

...There are three possible broad approaches to the conduct of interpersonal relations. The first is to consider one's self only and ride roughshod over others...The second...is always to put others before one's self...The third approach is the golden mean... The individual places himself first, but takes others into account.

— Joseph Wolpe

A look at some everyday situations will improve your understanding of the behavioral styles we've discussed. As you read the examples in this chapter, you may wish to pause and think about your own response before reading the alternative responses we have presented. These examples are oversimplified, of course, so we can demonstrate the ideas more clearly.

Dining Out

Adam and Evelyn are at dinner in a moderately expensive restaurant. Adam has ordered a rare steak; but when the steak is served, he finds it well-done. His action is:

Nonassertive: Adam grumbles to Evelyn about the "burned" meat, and vows that he won't patronize this restaurant in the future. He says nothing to the waitress, responding "Fine!" to her inquiry, "Is everything all right?"

His dinner and evening are spoiled, and he feels angry with himself for taking no action. Adam's estimate of himself and Evelyn's estimate of him are both deflated by the experience.

Aggressive: Adam angrily summons the waitress to his table. He berates her loudly and unfairly for not complying with his order. His actions ridicule the waitress and embarrass Evelyn. He demands and receives another steak, this one more to his liking. He feels in control of the situation, but Evelyn's embarrassment creates friction between them and spoils their night out. The waitress is humiliated and angry for the rest of the evening.

Assertive: Adam motions the waitress to his table. Noting that he had ordered a rare steak, he shows her the well-done meat. He asks politely but firmly that it be returned to the kitchen and replaced with the rare-cooked steak he originally requested. The waitress apologizes for the error, and shortly returns with a rare steak. Adam and Evelyn enjoy dinner and Adam feels satisfaction with himself. The waitress is pleased with a satisfied customer and a generous tip.

Something Borrowed

Helen is an airline flight attendant, bright, outgoing, and a good worker liked by customers and peers. She lives in a condo with two roommates, and is looking forward to a quiet evening at home one Friday when her roommate Mary asks a favor. Mary says that she is going out with a special man, and wants to borrow Helen's new and quite expensive necklace. The necklace was a gift from her brother, with whom Helen is very close, and it means a great deal to her. Her response is:

Nonassertive: She swallows her anxiety about loss or damage to the necklace. Although she feels that its special meaning makes it too personal to lend, she says "Sure!" She denies herself, rewards Mary for making an unreasonable request, and worries all evening.

Aggressive: Helen is outraged at her friend's request, tells her "Absolutely not!" and rebukes her severely for even daring to ask "such a stupid question." She humiliates Mary and makes a fool of herself too. Later she feels uncomfortable and guilty. Mary's hurt feelings show all evening, and she has a miserable time, which puzzles and dismays her date. Thereafter, the relationship between Helen and Mary becomes very strained.

Assertive: Helen explains the significance of the necklace to her roommate. Politely but firmly, she observes that the request is an unreasonable one since this piece of jewelry is particularly personal. Mary is disappointed but understanding, and Helen feels good for having been honest. Mary makes a big hit with her date just by being herself.

Have a Snort!

Pam is a friendly, socially active graduate student who has been going out with Paul, and has come to care a lot for him. One evening, he invites her to attend a small get-together with two other couples. As everyone gets acquainted at the party, Pam is enjoying herself. After an hour or so, one of the new friends brings out a small bag of cocaine. Everyone responds eagerly except Pam. She has not tried coke, and does not wish to experiment. She is in real conflict because Paul offers her a snort. She decides to be:

Nonassertive: She accepts the cocaine and pretends to have used it before. She carefully watches the others to see how they inhale the drug. She dreads the possibility they may ask her to take more, or to try freebasing. Pam is worried about what her friend is thinking about her. She has denied herself, been dishonest with Paul, and feels remorseful for giving in to something she did not wish to do.

Aggressive: Pam is visibly upset when offered the cocaine and blasts Paul for bringing her to a party of this "low type." She demands he take her home right away. When the others at the party say that she does not have to use if she doesn't wish to, she is not appeased. As she continues to behave indignantly, Paul is humiliated, embarrassed before his friends, and disappointed in her. Although he remains cordial toward Pam as he takes her home, he does not ask her out again.

Assertive: Pam does not accept the cocaine, replying simply, "No, thank you." She goes on to explain that she hasn't used the drug before and doesn't want to. She tells the group she'd rather go dancing this evening, but acknowledges their right to make their own choices. She asks Paul to take her home. (On the way, she makes clear to him her concern that he didn't tell her in advance that cocaine would be offered at the party. She emphasizes that he also had exposed her to possible arrest, had the party been discovered by the police. Pam considers breaking off her relationship with Paul.)

The Heavyweight

Barry and Madalynne, married nine years, have been having marital problems recently because he insists that she is overweight and needs to reduce. He brings the subject up continually, pointing out that she is no longer the woman he married (she was 25 pounds lighter then). He keeps telling her that such overweight is bad for her health, that she is a bad example for the children, and so on.

Barry teases Madalynne about being "chunky," looks

longingly at thin women, while commenting how attractive they look, and makes reference to her figure in front of their friends. Barry has been acting this way for the past three months and Madalynne is highly upset. She has been attempting to lose weight for those three months, but with little success. Following Barry's most recent rash of criticism, Madalynne is:

Nonassertive: She apologizes for her overweight, makes feeble excuses, or simply doesn't reply to some of Barry's comments. Internally, she feels both hostile toward her husband for his nagging, and guilty about being overweight. Her feelings of anxiety make it even more difficult for her to lose weight and the battle continues.

Aggressive: Madalynne goes into a long tirade about how her husband isn't any great bargain anymore, either! She brings up the fact that at night he falls asleep on the couch half the time, is a lousy sex partner, and doesn't pay enough attention to her. She complains that he humiliates her in front of the children and their close friends, and that he acts like a "lecherous old man" by the way he eyes other women. In her anger, she succeeds only in wounding Barry and driving a wedge between them by her counterattack.

Assertive: Approaching her husband when they are alone and will not be interrupted, Madalynne says that she feels that Barry is right about her need to lose weight, but she does not like the way he keeps after her about the problem. She points out that she is doing her best and is having a difficult time losing the weight and maintaining the loss. He admits that his harping is ineffective, and together they work out a plan in which he will systematically reinforce her for her efforts to lose weight.

The Neighbor Kid

Edmond and Virginia have a two-year-old boy and a baby girl. Over the last several nights, their neighbor's son, 17, has been sitting in his car, in his own driveway, with his car stereo blaring loudly. He begins just about the time their two young children go to bed on the side of the house where the boy plays the music. They have found it impossible to get the children to bed until the music stops. Edmond and Virginia are both disturbed and decide to be:

Nonassertive: They move the children into their own bedroom on the other side of the house, wait until the noise stops (around 1 a.m.), then transfer the children back to their own rooms. Then they go to bed much past their own usual bedtime. They quietly curse the teenager, and soon become alienated from their neighbors.

Aggressive: They call the police and protest that "one of those wild teenagers" next-door is creating a disturbance. They demand that the police put a stop to the noise at once. The police do talk with the boy and his parents, who get very angry as a result of their embarrassment about the police visit. They denounce Edmond and Virginia for reporting to the police without speaking to them first, and resolve to have nothing further to do with them.

Assertive: Edmond goes over to the boy's house and tells him that his stereo is keeping the children awake at night. Edmond suggests they try to work out an arrangement which allows the boy his music, but does not disturb the children's sleep. The boy reluctantly agrees to set a lower volume during the late hours, but he appreciates Edmond's cooperative attitude. Both parties feel good about the outcome, and agree to follow up a week later to be sure it is working as agreed.

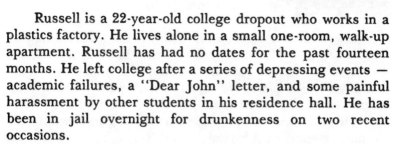

The Loser

Russell is a 22-year-old college dropout who works in a plastics factory. He lives alone in a small one-room, walk-up apartment. Russell has had no dates for the past fourteen months. He left college after a series of depressing events — academic failures, a "Dear John" letter, and some painful harassment by other students in his residence hall. He has been in jail overnight for drunkenness on two recent occasions.

Yesterday, Russell received a letter from his mother inquiring about his well-being, but primarily devoted to a discussion of his brother's recent successes. Today, his supervisor criticized him harshly for a mistake which was actually the supervisor's own fault. A secretary at the plant turned down his invitation to dinner.

When he arrived at his apartment that evening, feeling particularly depressed, his landlord met him at the door with a tirade about "drunken bums" and a demand that this month's rent be paid on time. Russell's response is:

Nonassertive: He takes on himself the burden of the landlord's attack, feeling added guilt and even greater depression. A sense of helplessness overcomes him. He wonders how his brother can be so successful while he considers himself so worthless. The secretary's rejection and the boss' criticism strengthen his conviction that he is "no damn good." Deciding the world would be a better place without him, he begins to think about how he will commit suicide.

Aggressive: The landlord has added the final straw to Russell's burden. He becomes extremely angry and pushes the landlord out of the way in order to get into his room. Once alone, he resolves to "get" the people who have been making his life so miserable recently: the supervisor, the secretary,

███████ and possibly others as well. He remembers the guns he saw in the pawn shop window yesterday.

Assertive: Russell responds firmly to the landlord, noting that he has paid his rent regularly, and that it is not due for another week. He reminds the landlord of a broken rail on the stairway and the plumbing repairs which were to have been accomplished weeks earlier. The following morning, after giving his life situation a great deal of thought, Russell calls the local mental health clinic to ask for help. At work, he approaches the supervisor calmly and explains the circumstances surrounding the mistake. Though somewhat defensive, the supervisor acknowledges her error and apologizes for her aggressive behavior.

Recognizing Your Own Nonassertive and Aggressive Behavior

The examples given in this chapter help to point out what "assertiveness" means in everyday events. Perhaps some of the situations "rang a bell" in your own life. Take a few minutes to honestly listen to yourself describe your relationships with others who are important to you. Carefully examine your contacts with parents, peers, co-workers, classmates, spouse, children, bosses, teachers, salespeople, neighbors, relatives. Who is dominant in these relationships? Are you easily taken advantage of in dealings with others? Do you usually express your feelings and ideas openly? Do you take advantage of or hurt others frequently?

Your responses to such questions provide hints which may lead you to explore in greater depth your assertive, nonassertive or aggressive behavior. In Chapter 7, you'll find a more systematic approach to such personal assessment, and a detailed "Assertiveness Inventory" for you to complete. We think you will find such self-examination rewarding, and a very important step toward increasing your interpersonal effectiveness.

6

"I Couldn't Think of What to Say!"

It takes two to speak truth — one to speak and another to hear.

— Henry David Thoreau

Self-expression is a universal human need. The form it takes is unique to each person, and consists of the several components of behavior described in this chapter. While individual differences make the world go 'round, each of us can learn the skills necessary for good communication. How effective is your self-expression?

Many people view assertiveness as a *verbal* behavior, believing that they must have just the right words to handle a situation effectively. We've found that *how* you express an assertive message is a good deal more important than *what* you say. Although popular with many assertiveness trainers, it has never been our style to offer scripts of "what to say when...." We are primarily concerned with encouraging honesty and directness, and much of that message is communicated *nonverbally*.

Participants in our groups and workshops have enjoyed watching us role-play a scene which makes this point clear: Bob is a dissatisfied customer who wishes to return a defective copy of *Everything You Always Wanted to Know About Assertiveness, But Were Too Timid To Ask* to the bookstore; Mike is the clerk. Using essentially the same words, "I bought this book here last week, and discovered that 20 pages are missing. I'd like a good copy or my money back," Bob approaches Mike in three different ways:

1. Bob walks slowly and hesitantly to the counter. His eyes are downcast at the floor, he speaks just above a whisper, his face looks as though it belongs on the cover of the book. He has a tight grip on the book, and a "please don't hurt me" posture.
2. Bob swaggers toward the counter, glares at Mike, addresses him in a voice heard all over the store. Bob's posture and fist-like gesture are an obvious attempt to intimidate the clerk.
3. Bob walks up to the counter facing Mike. He stands relaxed and erect, smiles, and looks directly at Mike with a friendly expression. In a conversational volume and tone of voice, he states the message, gesturing to point out the flaw in the book.

The three styles are over-exaggerated in our demonstration, of course, but the point is clear. The nonassertive, self-defeating style says to Mike that this customer is a pushover, and the slightest resistance will cause him to give up and go away. The second approach may achieve the goal of refund or exchange, but the aggressive Bob will leave with Mike's hostility directed at his back! With the assertive approach, Bob gets what he came for, and Mike feels good about having helped solve a problem for an appreciative customer.

The Components of Assertive Behavior

Systematic observations of assertive behavior have led behavioral scientists to conclude that there are several important components which contribute to an assertive act.

Our thinking in this area was significantly influenced by the late Michael Serber, a California psychiatrist who did extensive work with assertiveness training in the 1960s and 70s.

Let us examine the key components of assertive behavior in detail:

• *Eye Contact.* One of the most obvious aspects of behavior when talking to another person is where you look. If you look directly at the person as you speak, it helps to communicate your sincerity and to increase the directness of your message. If you look down or away much of the time, you present a lack of confidence, or a quality of deference to the other person. If you stare too intently, the other person may feel an uncomfortable invasion.

We do not advocate that you maximize eye contact. Continuously looking at someone can make the other person uncomfortable, is inappropriate and unnecessary, and may appear to be a game. Moreover, eye contact is a cultural variable; many cultural groups limit the amount of eye contact which is acceptable, particularly between age groups or members of the opposite sex. Nevertheless, the importance of eye contact is obvious. A relaxed and steady gaze at the other, looking away occasionally as is comfortable, helps to make conversation more personal, to show interest in and respect for the other person, and to enhance the directness of your message.

As is true with other behaviors, eye contact may be improved by conscious effort, in small steps. Be aware of your eyes as you talk with others, and attempt to gradually optimize your eye attention in conversation.

• *Body Posture.* As you watch other people talking with each other, carefully observe how each is standing or sitting. You may be as amazed as we have been by the number of people who talk with someone while their bodies are turned

away from that person. People sitting side by side often turn
only their heads toward one another while talking. Next time
you are in that situation, notice how much more personal the
conversation becomes with a slight turn of the torso — say 30
degrees — toward the other person.

Relative "power" in an encounter may be emphasized by
standing or sitting. A particularly evident power imbalance
may be seen in the relationship between a tall adult and a
small child; the adult who is thoughtful enough to bend or
crouch to the child's height will find an observable difference
in the quality of communication, and usually a much more
responsive child!.

In a situation in which you are called upon to stand up for
yourself, it may be useful to do just that — stand up. An
active and erect posture, while facing the other person
directly, lends additional assertiveness to your message. A
slumped, passive stance gives the other person an immediate
advantage, as does any tendency on your part to lean back or
move away. Remember Bob's first approach to the bookstore
clerk?

• *Distance/Physical Contact.* An interesting aspect of
cross-cultural research into nonverbal communication is that
of distance vs. closeness between people in conversation. As a
rough guide, it may be said that, among European peoples,
the farther North one goes, the farther apart individuals stand
when engaged in conversation. In the United States, as in
Europe, closeness seems to increase in warmer climates; but
there are important exceptions, notably among ethnic
subcultures which value closeness and contact differently.

Closeness is, of course, not necessarily related to
temperature. Cultural and social customs are products of very
complex historical factors. It is fascinating, for example, to
contrast the almost obligatory, polite distance present in the
queue for a London bus, with the pushing, shoving body
contact which is part of the cloakroom scramble at a winter

play in Moscow! In the Arab world, it is customary for men to greet one another with a hug and kiss, and to stand very close to each other. Interestingly, it would be considered very inappropriate for an Arab man to behave toward a woman in this way, yet that is quite common in the United States and Southern Europe.

Distance from another person does have a considerable effect upon communication. Standing or sitting very closely, or touching, suggests intimacy in a relationship, unless the people happen to be in a crowd or very cramped quarters. The typical discomfort of elevator passengers is a classic example of the difficulty we have in dealing with closeness! Coming too close may offend the other person, make him/her defensive, or open the door to greater intimacy. It can be worthwhile to check out verbally how the other person feels about your closeness.

• *Gestures.* Accentuating your message with appropriate gestures can add emphasis, openness, and warmth. Bob Alberti traces his use of gestures in conversation to his Italian heritage. While enthusiastic gesturing is indeed a somewhat culturally-related behavior, a relaxed use of gestures can add depth or power to your messages. Uninhibited movement can also suggest openness, self-confidence (unless the gesturing is erratic and nervous), and spontaneity on the part of the speaker.

• *Facial Expression.* Ever see someone trying to express anger while smiling or laughing? It just doesn't come across. Effective assertions require an expression that agrees with the message. An angry message is clearest when delivered with a straight, non-smiling countenance. A friendly communication should not be delivered with a dark frown. Let your face say the same thing your words are saying!

If you will look at yourself in the mirror, you can learn a great deal about what your face says on your behalf. First, relax all the muscles of your face as much as you can. Let go of your expression, relax the muscles around your mouth, let your jaw go loose, let your cheeks soften, along with the wrinkles of your forehead and around your eyes. Pay careful attention to the relaxed, soft feelings. Now smile, bringing your mouth up as widely as you can. Feel the tightness in your cheeks, around your eyes, all the way up to your ears. Hold that smile, look at the expression in the mirror, and concentrate on the feelings of tightness. Now relax your face completely again. Notice the difference between the relaxed feelings and those of the tight smile, and the difference between the expressions you see in the mirror.

With greater awareness of how your facial muscles feel in various expressions, and of how you look when you smile and when you are relaxed, you can begin to control your facial expression more consciously, and to make it congruent with what you are thinking, feeling, or saying. And you may develop a more natural, less "plastic" smile for those times when you really want your happiness to show!

• *Voice Tone, Inflection, Volume.* The way we use our voices is a vital element in our communications. The same words spoken through clenched teeth in anger offer an entirely different message than when they are shouted with joy or whispered in fear.

A level, well modulated, conversational statement is convincing without being intimidating. A whispered monotone will seldom convince another person that you mean business, while a shouted epithet will bring defenses into the path of communication.

Voice is one of the easiest of the components of behavior on which to gain accurate feedback these days. Most everyone has easy access to a small cassette recorder which can be used to "try out" different styles of your voice. You may wish to experiment with a conversational tone, an angry shouted blast, a caring message, a persuasive argument. You may be surprised at how quiet your "shouts" are, or at how loud your "conversational tone" is.

Consider at least three dimensions of your voice:

tone (is it raspy, whiny, seductively soft, angry?);

inflection (do you emphasize certain syllables, as in a question, or speak in a monotone, or with "sing-song" effect?);

volume (do you try to gain attention with a whisper or to overpower others with loudness, or is it very difficult for you to shout even when you want to?).

If you can control and use your voice effecitvely, you have acquired a powerful tool in your self-expression. Practice with a recorder, trying out different styles until you achieve a style you like. Allow time for changes to come, and use the recorder regularly to check your progress.

● *Fluency*. Psychiatrist Mike Serber employed an exercise he called "sell me something," in which he asked the client to talk persuasively about an object, such as a watch, for thirty seconds. For many people, it is very difficult to put together a string of words lasting thirty seconds.

A smooth flow of speech is a valuable asset to get your point across in any type of conversation. It is not necessary to talk rapidly for a long period; but if your speech is interrupted with long periods of hesitation, your listeners may get bored, and will probably recognize you are very unsure of yourself. Clear and slow comments are more easily understood and more powerful than rapid speech which is erratic and filled with long pauses and stammering.

Once again, the tape recorder is a valuable tool. Use the machine to practice by talking on a familiar subject for thirty seconds. Then listen to yourself, noticing pauses of three seconds or more and space fillers such as "uhhh..." and "you know...." Repeat the same exercise, more slowly if necessary, trying to eliminate any significant pauses. Gradually increase the difficulty of the task by dealing with less familiar topics, trying to be persuasive, pretending to respond in an argument, or working with a friend to keep a genuine dialog going. The program of the Toastmasters organization offers a unique opportunity for practice with feedback from a supportive audience.

• *Timing.* In general, we advocate spontaneity of expression as a goal. Hesitation may diminish the effectiveness of your assertions, but it is never "too late" to be assertive! Even though the ideal moment has passed, you will usually find it worthwhile to go to the person at a later time and express your feelings. Indeed, it is so important to express one's feelings that psychologists have developed special techniques to help individuals express strong emotions toward those who may have died (e.g., parents) before the feelings could be expressed.

Spontaneous assertion will help keep your life clear, and will help you to focus accurately on the feelings you have at the time. Nevertheless, at times it is necessary to choose an occasion to discuss a strong feeling. It is not a good idea to confront someone in front of a group, for example, because extra defenses are sure to be present under those conditions.

• *Listening.* This component is perhaps the most difficult both to describe and to change, yet it may well be the most important. Assertive listening involves an active commitment to the other person. It requires your full attention, and calls for no overt act on your part, although eye contact and certain gestures — such as nodding — are often appropriate. Listening demonstrates your respect for the other person. It requires that you avoid expressing *yourself* for a time, yet is not a nonassertive act.

Listening is not simply the physical response of hearing sounds — indeed, deaf persons may be excellent "listeners." Effective listening may involve giving feedback to the other person, so that it is clear that you understood what was said.

Assertive listening requires at least these elements:

tuning in to the other person, by stopping other activities, turning off the tv, ignoring other distractions, focusing your energy in his or her direction;

attending to the message, by making eye contact if possible, nodding to show that you hear, perhaps touching her or him; and

actively attempting to *understand* before responding, by thinking about the underlying message — the feelings behind the words — rather than trying to interpret, or to come up with an answer.

Assertiveness includes respect for the rights and feelings of others. That means assertive *receiving* — sensitivity to others — as well as assertive *sending*.

As with other components of assertive behavior, listening is a skill that can be learned. It is hard work, takes patience, and requires other people willing to work with you. You may find it useful to hook up with a "practice partner," to take turns listening to each other and sharpening each other's listening skills. Practice accurate paraphrasing of each other's communications. It will strengthen your capacity to listen.

Good listening will make all of your assertions more effective, and will contribute much to the quality of your relationships.

• *Thoughts.* Another component of assertiveness which escapes direct observation is the thinking process. Although it has long been understood intuitively that attitudes influence behavior, only recently has psychological research been sophisticated enough to deal directly with the link. Psychologists Albert Ellis of New York City and Donald Meichenbaum of Ontario, Canada, and psychiatrist Aaron Beck of Philadelphia have been particularly influential in focusing attention on the cognitive dimensions of behavior.

Ellis has reduced the process to a simple A-B-C: (A) an event takes place; (B) a person sees and interprets it internally; (C) the person reacts in some way. Part B — the perception and thought process — is what we have tended to ignore in the past. More recent developments in the field of "cognitive behavior therapy" have produced specific procedures for developing assertive thinking. Thus you can now work on your thoughts as well as your eye contact, posture, and gestures.

Thinking, of course, is probably the most complex thing we humans do. As you might imagine, procedures for changing our thoughts and attitudes are very complex also. We will discuss this area more in Chapter 9, but for now, consider two aspects of your assertive thinking: your attitudes about whether it is a good idea in general for people to be assertive, and your thoughts about yourself when you are in a situation which calls for assertive action. Some people, for instance, think it is not a good idea for *anybody* to express themselves. And some say it's okay for *others,* but not for *me.* If either of these beliefs rings a bell with you, we want you to pay particular attention to Chapter 9 and work on thinking assertively!

• *Content:* We save this obvious dimension of assertiveness for last to emphasize that, although *what* you say is clearly important, it is often *less* important than most of us generally believe. We encourage honest and spontaneous expression. That means saying forcefully, "I'm damn mad about what you just did!" rather than, "You're an S.O.B.!" Many people hesitate because they don't know *what* to say. Others have found the practice of saying *something* about their feelings at the time to be a valuable step.

We encourage you to express yourself — and to take responsibility for your feelings; don't blame the other person for how you feel. Note the difference in the above example between "I'm mad" and "You're an S.O.B." It is not necessary to put the other person down (aggressive) in order to express your feeling (assertive).

You can imagine a wide variety of situations which show the importance of *how* you make yourself heard. The time you spend thinking about just the right words would be better spent making those assertions! The ultimate goal is expressing yourself, honestly and spontaneously, in a manner right for you.

Mississippi psychologists Myles Cooley and James Hollandsworth have developed a "components" model for assertive statements, made up of seven elements which are grouped into three general categories. They suggest that *saying "no" or taking a stand* includes stating your position, explaining your reason, and expressing understanding. *Asking favors or asserting rights* may be expressed by stating the problem, making a request, and getting clarification. Finally, *expressing feelings* is accomplished by a statement of your emotions in a situation. (You may find it valuable to practice each of these types of statements with your practice partner, or into a tape recorder.)

Assertiveness does not depend upon being highly verbal, but some folks do seem to have difficulty finding the "right words." We do not advocate particular formulas or scripts for assertive expression, preferring to encourage you to use your own language, and to recognize that the *style* of your delivery is more important than the words anyway. Words are important, of course, and many people do stumble over vocabulary. Often, however, clients tell us clearly how they feel about a particular situation, and then ask, "What shall I say to the person?" Our answer: "The same thing you just told me!"

One further word about content. Psychologist Donald Cheek, a neighbor and former colleague of ours, has pointed out the need to adapt assertiveness to your cultural setting. Particularly for minorities who may find themselves in "survival" situations, he suggests that *what* you say must take into consideration *to whom* you are saying it! Language which would be interpreted as assertive within one's own subculture, for example, could easily be interpreted as aggressive by "outsiders."

We do not advocate that you change yourself to adapt to whatever any situation seems to invite. Nevertheless, all of us *do* deal with individuals differently, depending upon our respective roles and the perceived "power" of others over us. We hope you can be yourself; honesty remains the best overall guide.

It is not usually the content that hangs people up. It is the anxiety, or the lack of skills, or the belief that "I have no right..."

We hope this chapter has caused you to think more systematically about your own self-expression. Be sure to note in your log the ways these components of behavior are important to you, and begin to formulate some goals for your own work in assertiveness. You'll probably want to go back over this material once or twice, until the components are familiar to you. In the next chapter, you'll begin to assess your own assertive strengths and weaknesses.

7

Measuring Your Assertiveness

There is no greatness where there is not simplicity, goodness, and truth.

— Leo Tolstoi

What do you know about your own assertiveness?

Others' reactions give you clues: Aunt Jane says, "You're sassy!" The boss tells you to be more forceful with customers. Or perhaps the children believe you need to "tell off" the mechanic. Maybe you tried to speak up to a clerk, who responded with a scornful look.

While everyday comments and reactions such as these are helpful indications of your progress in assertiveness, we hope you'll be more thorough and systematic in observing yourself.

We should first point out to you that *measuring* assertiveness is one of the toughest problems trainers and trainees have faced since assertiveness training got started. Many, many tests have been developed. None really does the job thoroughly and accurately.

The real problem, of course, is that assertiveness itself is such an elusive concept. There is no one single human characteristic you can put a finger on and say, "*That's* assertiveness!" It is a complex phenomenon, which depends on both the persons involved and the particular situation.

A thorough assessment of assertiveness would be based on a more adequate definition of the concept than we currently have. And it would take into account the four dimensions we have discussed: situations, attitudes, behaviors, obstacles. A simple paper-and-pencil test can hardly do justice to that complex task!

That doesn't mean, however, that we ought to abandon all efforts to figure out how we're doing in assertive self-expression. It can be very valuable to take a systematic look at your life and identify areas of strength and weakness. Just don't try to lump those all together and say, "I scored 73. I must be pretty assertive!"

Take a few minutes right now to respond to the "Assertiveness Inventory" below. Be honest with yourself! After you complete the Inventory, read on for the discussion of results, and for specific steps to follow to make the results practical. The Inventory is not a "psychological test," so just relax and enjoy this brief exploration of your ability to express yourself appropriately.

THE ASSERTIVENESS INVENTORY

The following questions will be helpful in assessing your assertiveness. Be honest in your responses. All you have to do is draw a circle around the number that describes you best. For some questions the assertive end of the scale is at 0, for others at 4. Key: 0 means **no** or **never**; 1 means **somewhat** or **sometimes**; 2 means **average**; 3 means **usually** or **a good deal**; and 4 means **practically always** or **entirely**.

1. When a person is highly unfair, do you call it to attention? 0 1 2 3 4
2. Do you find it difficult to make decisions? 0 1 2 3 4
3. Are you openly critical of others ideas, opinions, behavior? 0 1 2 3 4
4. Do you speak out in protest when someone takes your place in line? 0 1 2 3 4
5. Do you often avoid people or situations for fear of embarassment? 0 1 2 3 4
6. Do you usually have confidence in your own judgment? 0 1 2 3 4

7. Do you insist that your spouse or roommate take on a fair share of household chores?........................0 1 2 3 4
8. Are you prone to "fly off the handle?".....................0 1 2 3 4
9. When a salesman makes an effort, do you find it hard to say "No" even though the merchandise is not really what you want? 0 1 2 3 4
10. When a latecomer is waited on before you are, do you call attention to the situation?..........................0 1 2 3 4
11. Are you reluctant to speak up in a discussion or debate?..0 1 2 3 4
12. If a person has borrowed money (or a book, garment, thing of value) and is overdue in returning it, do you mention it?...0 1 2 3 4
13. Do you continue to pursue an argument after the other person has had enough?..........................0 1 2 3 4
14. Do you generally express what you feel? 0 1 2 3 4
15. Are you disturbed if someone watches you at work? 0 1 2 3 4
16. If someone keeps kicking or bumping your chair in a movie or a lecture, do you ask the person to stop?.........0 1 2 3 4
17. Do you find it difficult to keep eye contact when talking to another person? 0 1 2 3 4
18. In a good restaurant, when your meal is improperly prepared or served, do you ask the waiter/waitress to correct the situation?.................................0 1 2 3 4
19. When you discover merchandise is faulty, do you return it for an adjustment? 0 1 2 3 4
20. Do you show your anger by name-calling or obscenities?...0 1 2 3 4
21. Do you try to be a wallflower or a piece of the furniture in social situations?..................................0 1 2 3 4
22. Do you insist that your property manager (mechanic, repairman, etc.) make repairs, adjustments or replacements which are his/her responsibility?..............0 1 2 3 4
23. Do you often step in and make decisions for others?.......0 1 2 3 4
24. Are you able openly to express love and affection? 0 1 2 3 4
25. Are you able to ask your friends for small favors or help?...0 1 2 3 4
26. Do you think you always have the right answer?...........0 1 2 3 4
27. When you differ with a person you respect, are you able to speak up for your own viewpoint?.....................0 1 2 3 4
28. Are you able to refuse unreasonable requests made by friends? 0 1 2 3 4
29. Do you have difficulty complimenting or praising others? 0 1 2 3 4
30. If you are disturbed by someone smoking near you, can you say so?......................................0 1 2 3 4
31. Do you shout or use bullying tactics to get others to do as you wish?.......................................0 1 2 3 4
32. Do you finish other people's sentences for them? 0 1 2 3 4
33. Do you get into physical fights with others, especially with strangers? 0 1 2 3 4
34. At family meals, do you control the conversation?.........0 1 2 3 4
35. When you meet a stranger, are you the first to introduce yourself and begin a conversation? 0 1 2 3 4

Readers and assertiveness trainees have some common reactions when they complete the Inventory.

"I hate tests!"

"The questions are easy to figure out. I could have cheated."

"I didn't feel well when I took it."

Such an inventory is necessarily general. You may have found that some items don't apply to your life. Unfortunately, you can't talk to the questions:

"What does that mean?"

"It depends on the situation"

"Some days I feel moody and find it hard to be assertive."

Nevertheless, when you take the time to answer the relevant questions honestly, the Inventory can be a helpful tool in your growth in assertiveness.

"Whadjaget?"

When you complete the Inventory, you'll probably be tempted to add up your total score. *Don't!* It really has no meaning. There is no such thing as a *general* quality of assertiveness. As you will recall from earlier chapters, and as you have no doubt experienced in your own life, "what is assertive" must be answered in terms of the person and the situation.

The Inventory, as we noted above, is not a standardized psychological test; the studies required to thoroughly evaluate and approve a test have not been conducted. Thus, a "total score" approach is not appropriate.

Analyzing Your Results

We suggest the following steps for analysis of your responses to the Assertiveness Inventory:

• Look at individual events in your life, involving particular people or groups, and consider your strengths and shortcomings accordingly.

• Look at your responses to questions 1, 2, 4, 5, 6, 7, 9, 10, 11, 12, 14, 15, 16, 17, 18, 19, 21, 22, 24, 25, 27, 28, 30, and 35. These questions are oriented toward *nonassertive* behavior. Do your answers to these items tell you that you are rarely speaking up for yourself? Or are there perhaps some specific situations which give you trouble?

• Look at your responses to questions 3, 8, 13, 20, 23, 26, 29, 31, 32, 33, and 34. These questions are oriented toward *aggressive* behavior. Do your answers to these questions suggest you are pushing others around more than you realized?

• Most people confirm from completing these three steps that assertiveness is *situational* in their lives. No one is nonassertive *all* the time, aggressive *all* the time, assertive *all* the time! Each person behaves in each of the three ways at various times, depending upon the situation. It is possible that you have a *characteristic style* that leans heavily in one direction. You may discover your "Achilles Heel," and by so doing, begin the necessary change process.

• Re-read each question on the Inventory and write out in your log a discussion of your feelings about the item. An example:

Question 1. *When a person is highly unfair, do you call it to attention?*

Response: *0*

Discussion: *I'm afraid that if I said anything, the other person would become very angry. Perhaps I'd lose a friend, or maybe the person would yell at me. That would upset me a lot.*

• Go over all of the information you have generated from the preceding steps, and begin drawing some general conclusions. Look specifically at four aspects of the information:

...What *situations* give you trouble? And which can you handle easily?

...What are your *attitudes* about expressing yourself? Does it generally feel ''right'' to you?

...What *obstacles* are in the way of your assertions? Are you frightened of the consequences? Do other people in your life make it especially difficult?

...Are your *behavior skills* up to the job? Can you be expressive when you need to?

Examine these four areas carefully. Write comments in your log, summarizing your observations of yourself. If you'll spend some time now, thinking about these aspects of your own style of self-expression, it will help you to see your own needs more clearly, to set goals for yourself, and to determine where to go from here in your assertiveness training program.

HOW ARE YOU DOING?

From time to time throughout *Your Perfect Right,* we've inserted this ''break'' in the text to get you to pause and take stock. No big formal deal — just a periodic checkup to help you stay on track.

Take some time now to answer the questions below. Be honest with yourself, and let the answers guide your next steps.

• Have you read and understood all the material in the previous chapters?

• Do our explanations and examples fit with your own experience?

   If not, can you adapt them to your needs?

• Are you doing the exercises and answering the questions we have raised?

• Has ''assertiveness'' begun to mean something real to you?

• Have you set some preliminary goals for your growth in assertiveness?

• Are you keeping a log of your progress?

• Have you asked for help if you need it for anxiety or other obstacles?

• Have you identified your own shortcomings in assertiveness: anxiety, attitudes, social skills?

8

Goal For It!

*Never play another person's game. Play your
own.*

— Andrew Salter

A professor of ours used to tell his graduate students that
changing yourself is like planning a trip: you have to find out
where you are now, decide where you want to go, then figure
out how to get *there* from *here*.

Much of the material in this book so far has been devoted
to helping you find out where you are now in relation to
assertiveness. In the following chapters we'll be focussing on
ways to "get there." This chapter is the bridge — to help you
decide where you're headed. Setting your goals may be the
most important and most difficult step of all.

"How Do I Know What I Want?"

Assertiveness training evolved out of the idea that people live better lives if they can express what they want, if they can let others know how they would like to be treated. Some folks, however, find it hard to really know what they want from life. If you have spent most of your life doing for others, and believing that what you want is not important, it can be quite a chore to get a handle on just what is important to you!

Some people do seem to know exactly how they feel and what they want. If the neighbor's dog is barking loudly, the feeling may be annoyance or anger or fear, but such people are able to translate the feeling, get to the key issue at hand and make the needed assertions, if any.

Others find it difficult to know what their feelings are and what they want to accomplish in an encounter. They often hesitate to be assertive, lamenting "Assert *what?* I don't know what I want!" If you have such trouble you may find it valuable to try to *label* your feelings. Anger, anxiety, boredom, discomfort, and fear are common feelings. Among others you will experience are happiness, irritation, love, relaxation, sadness.

Some people will require only a few moments reflection to reveal what is being felt inside. Others may need a more active first step. It often helps to say *something* to the people involved: "I'm upset, but I'm not sure why." Or perhaps, "I'm feeling depressed." "Something feels wrong, but I can't put my finger on it." Such a statement will start you on an active search for the feeling you're sensing, and will help begin to clarify your goals.

Perhaps it is a fear of some sort which is preventing you from recognizing your feelings — a type of protective mechanism. Or you may just be so far out of touch with your feelings that you have virtually forgotten what they mean. Don't bog down at this stage. Go ahead and try to express yourself. You will probably become aware of your goal even as you proceed. Indeed, maybe all you wanted was to express something! If you do begin to recognize the underlying feeling and decide to change directions in mid-stream ("I started out angry, but realized that what I really wanted was attention!"), that is a constructive step!

You can go a long way toward clarifying your feelings in a specific situation by identifying your general life goals. Assertiveness does need direction; while it seems to be a good idea in general, it is of little value for its own sake!

You will find at times that goals will be in conflict. You may wish, for example, to keep a friendly relationship with your next door neighbor, but *also* wish to quiet his noisy dog. If you confront him about the dog, you may risk the good relationship. At such a point, clarification of your own goals will be invaluable in deciding what to do, and how to do it.

A Behavioral Model for Personal Growth

Dr. Carl Rogers is recognized as the most influential psychological thinker of the twentieth century. His ideas were the major influence in the development of the "human potential movement." The list on the following two pages was prepared by Dr. Alberti in the early 1970s, in an attempt to translate Dr. Rogers' ideas into specific behaviors which could be carried out. We think you'll find it helpful, as you consider this matter of goals for your own growth, to read and ponder the *Behavioral Model for Personal Growth*.

A BEHAVIORAL MODEL FOR PERSONAL GROWTH
Robert E. Alberti, Ph.D.

Dr. Carl Rogers, in his book, *On Becoming A Person,* identified three major characteristics of healthy personal growth. The following "behavioral model" is based on the three qualities identified by Rogers.

"An Increasing Openness to Experience"
How recently have you
- participated in a new sport or game?
- changed your views on an important (political, personal, professional) issue?
- tried a new hobby or craft?
- taken a course in a new field?
- studied a new language or culture?
- spent fifteen minutes or more paying attention to your body feelings, senses (relaxation, tension, sensuality)?
- listened for fifteen minutes or more to a religious, political, professional, or personal viewpoint with which you disagreed?
- tasted a new food, smelled a new odor, listened to a new sound?
- allowed yourself to cry? or to say "I care about you"? or to laugh until you cried? or to scream at the top of your lung capacity? or to admit you were afraid?
- watched the sun (or moon) rise or set? or a bird soar on the wind's currents? or a flower open to the sun?
- traveled to a place you had never been before?
- made a new friend? or cultivated an old friendship?
- spent an hour or more really communicating (actively listening and responding honestly) with a person of a different cultural or racial background?
- taken a "fantasy trip" — allowing your imagination to run freely for ten minutes to an hour or more?

"Increasingly Existential Living"

How recently have you

• done something you felt like doing at that moment, without regard for the consequences?

• stopped to "listen" to what was going on inside you?

• spontaneously expressed a feeling — anger, joy, fear, sadness, caring — without thinking about it?

• done what you wanted to, instead of what you thought you "should" do?

• allowed yourself to spend time or money on an immediate payoff rather than saving for tomorrow?

• bought something you wanted on impulse?

• done something no one (including you) expected you to do?

"An Increasing Trust in One's Organism"

How recently have you

• done what felt right to you, against the advice of others?

• allowed yourself to experiment creatively with new approaches to old problems?

• expressed an unpopular opinion assertively in the face of majority opposition?

• used your own intellectual reasoning ability to work out a solution to a difficult problem?

• made a decision and acted upon it right away?

• acknowledged by your actions that you can direct your own life?

• cared enough about yourself to get a physical exam (within two years)?

• told others of your religious faith, or philosophy of life?

• assumed a position of leadership in your profession, or an organization, or your community?

• asserted your feelings when you were treated unfairly?

• risked sharing your personal feelings with another person?

• designed and/or built something on your own?

• admitted you were wrong?

Structuring Your Goals

OK, let's get specific. You want to write in your log a few goals which will help guide your work on assertiveness in the weeks to come.

Start by thinking creatively about what you want to get out of this program of personal growth. Brainstorm about your assertiveness, writing down anything that comes to mind. Write quickly. Don't ignore or criticize any idea, no matter how silly it may seem. Be as open-minded as you can.

After you have compiled a list of possibilities, you'll need to pare it down into a short list of specific goals. What should go into that list? Consider six key criteria as you decide: *Personal factors, ideals, feasibility, flexibility, time,* and *priorities.* Make each of your own goals "qualify" in terms of those six factors:

Personal factors

As you evaluate your specific goals for assertive growth, use your discoveries about yourself from the Assertiveness Inventory and your log entries.

In Chapter 3, "Your Personal Growth Log," we suggested that you keep track of your assertive behavior using four categories:

- *Situations* that were difficult or easy for you.
- Your *attitudes* about expressing yourself.
- *Obstacles* to your assertiveness, such as certain people or fears.
- The *skills* you possess relating to assertive behavior, such as eye contact, voice volume, gestures.

Spend some time now reviewing your log, looking for ideas which will help you to define goals for yourself.

Ideals

There are probably many people you admire. If you select the qualities of one or more "models" of assertiveness as ideals toward which you can strive, you'll have some specific

ready in mind. A well-chosen ideal will
to your goals.

82, the *ASSERT* newsletter selected well
es for an ''Assertive Person of the Year''
ividuals received the award, given for
>nal and career achievement which
icept of assertiveness: motion picture and
n Alda, women's rights activist Sonia
ear freeze campaigner Randall Forsberg.
ot agree with these choices, but you can
ons who exhibit the kind of assertiveness
r.

A good model may be a best friend, a beloved teacher, a
public figure, or someone of historical importance. This
person's behavior can be one basis for your goals. Think
about the qualities she has that you want to attain. Key in on
such areas as self-confidence, courage, persistence, honesty.
Measure your behavior against the model you choose, and
think often about the person. Let your reflection on your
model's behavior give you energy to keep at your own process
of improvement in assertiveness.

Feasibility

As we have suggested at various points in *Your Perfect
Right*, proceed at achieving your changes in assertive
behavior slowly and in small steps to increase your chances of
success. Don't set your goals too high and risk early failure.
Instead, do a little each day, advancing step by step.

Author/philosopher Morton Hunt illustrates this
admonition in a poignant way. He tells the story of how he
learned to cope with major life stresses by remembering a
harrowing experience at age eight. Hunt and several friends
climbed a cliff near his home. Half way up, he got very scared
and could go no further. He was caught: to think of going
either up or down overwhelmed him. The others left him
behind as darkness approached.

Eventually his father came to the rescue, but Morton had to do the work! His father talked him down, and the pattern was established to overcome future fearfulness. The advice was timeless... "take one step at a time", "go inch by inch," "don't worry about what comes next," "don't look way ahead."

Later in life, when faced with major fearful events, Morton Hunt remembered that simple lesson: don't look at the dire consequences; start with the first small step and let that small success provide the courage to take another and another. The small-step goals will add up until the major goal is accomplished.

The suggestions Hunt's father gave are an excellent approach to growth in assertiveness. Continually remind yourself to break your major goals into small, manageable steps. Take your time. Soon the end will be in sight; you will notice changes in yourself. And you will reach your goals, one step at a time.

Flexibility

Deciding whether and how you'd like to change can be a complex and never-ending process. Goals are never "set"; they are constantly changing as you and your life circumstances change.

Maybe at one time you wanted to finish school, and when you did, suddenly a whole new range of possibilities opened up. Or perhaps you sought to make $20,000 a year; by the time you reached that level you needed $40,000! Then there was that promotion; when you got it, you found you didn't like your new responsibilities as well as your old.

So *change* itself is the constant factor. And the key to successful goal setting is to keep your goals flexible enough that you can adapt to the inevitable changes which will come in your life.

Time

In their *Relaxation & Stress Reduction Workbook*, Martha Davis, Elizabeth Robbins Eshelman and Matthew McKay suggest listing your goals according to how long it will take to accomplish them. While Davis, Eshelman and McKay employ this method for all types of life goals, we will focus here only on assertiveness goals. Here are some examples:

Long Range Goals
- Behave more assertively with my spouse.
- Increase my adventuresome or risk-taking behavior.
- Reduce my tension/anxiety about behaving assertively.
- Overcome my fear of conflict and anger.
- Gain a good understanding of how my childhood experiences influenced my assertiveness.

One Year Goals
- Compliment those close to me more frequently.
- Speak out in front of groups more often.
- Say no and mean it!
- Improve my eye contact while being assertive.
- Don't say "I'm sorry" or "I hate to bother you" so much.

One Month Goals
- Return the faulty vacuum cleaner to the store.
- Say no to the finder of committee members at work.
- Get tougher in disciplining my children.
- Spend a night on the town with my spouse.
- Start listening to audio tapes on assertiveness.

These lists are only ideas from hundreds or thousands of possibilities! Develop your own unique, personal lists. Be assertive! No one knows your needs better than you.

Priorities

After developing your short range, mid-range, and long range lists of goals, give some thought to your own priorities. Identify "top, middle and bottom drawer" goals:

Top Drawer — goals which are most important.

Middle Drawer — goals which are important, but don't need to be accomplished right away.

Bottom Drawer — those goals which can be put off indefinitely without causing great stress.

If you'll select two top drawer goals from each of the three time lists, you'll have six top priority items to work on during a period of one month. Each month you can select a new list. Some goals will stay top drawer, others won't.

Goal For It!

You have identified some possible goals for your growth, evaluated them, and begun to sort them according to their importance and feasibility. You are ready to select — and write in your log — a few goals to work on over the next weeks and months. Throw out the ideas that are too far-fetched or out of reach for you at this time. Be practical at this point. Narrow down exactly what your next steps will be in your assertiveness journey.

As you proceed in your choice-making process, keep in mind your model/ideal person. See if your choices generally agree with those qualities you wish to develop. Your assertive behavior won't exactly match that of your ideal — in fact, you don't want it to. You are trying to be the person you really are, not someone else.

Remember that your choices are always tentative and subject to change with new circumstances and information. Stay on your course, but remain flexible, making adjustments as needed. Setting goals for your own life can be an exciting process. As you take steps toward each goal, you'll find a genuine sense of accomplishment in your progress. Pat yourself on the back as you achieve each step. Use your log regularly to keep track. And most important: *let this be for you*. Your goals needn't please anybody else. By paying careful attention to your own desires and needs, you'll be playing your own game. And that's the only one that counts.

9

Don't Let Your Thoughts Stop You!

If a person continues to see only giants, it means he is still looking at the world through the eyes of a child.

— Anais Nin

"O.K.," you say, "maybe I'm not as assertive as I'd like to be. You can't teach an old dog new tricks. That's just the way I am. I can't change it."

We don't agree. Hundreds of thousands of people have found that it was possible for them to change. Becoming more assertive is a learning process, and it takes longer for some of us. But the process is not really that difficult, and the rewards are great.

Right *thinking* about assertiveness is crucial. Thoughts, beliefs, attitudes, and feelings set the stage for behavior. Your mind needs to be free to respond to each new situation calling for assertive action. Faulty attitudes, beliefs, and thoughts hold you back and stop your natural flow. "You are what you think" even more than "you are what you eat." Your thoughts will be a great resource to help you generate greater assertiveness if you will rid yourself of counterproductive thinking!

In this chapter, you will find some "pep talks" and some specific procedures which will help you to look at your thinking process in relation to assertiveness. Consider carefully what is said here. We are probably going to challenge some of your beliefs about how life works.

Your Attitude Toward Becoming Assertive

Perhaps you, like many folks, have for most of your life experienced parents, teachers and peers, saying, "You have *no right....*" Now we are telling you, "You have a *perfect right...,*" that it is *good,* it is *right,* it is *okay* to assert yourself. How to deal with these conflicting messages? Trust yourself. Experiment a little. You owe it to yourself to try!

Your capacity to grow in assertiveness will be helped or hindered by your attitude. If you'll cooperate with the natural process of self-expression, you can learn to enjoy each new challenge. Don't let negative attitudes stunt your growth.

One common negative response is to imagine all the "dire consequences" which may result from taking risks in your relationships. ("Oh, dear. What might happen?") Recognize that at times it is appropriate to ignore those excessive cautions, and take just one small step toward your goal. Life is not likely to present you with any task you cannot handle.

You can take charge of your own growth process, and guide your development in a positive, assertive direction. You'll find your attitudes can change as a *result* of your actions. Positive responses from others, better feeling about yourself, and accomplishment of your goals will reward you for expressing yourself and standing up for your rights. Pay attention to these positive results; they offer important support and encouragement as you practice new skills.

Your Attitude Toward Yourself

Can you express the feeling of elation you get when you achieve a highly valued personal goal, such as completing a college course or a remodeling job on your home? Do you allow yourself the pleasure of feeling satisfied with a job well done? How about when you do something which makes someone else happy? Can you congratulate yourself when you succeed? When you fail, can you accept your foibles with honesty and laugh at yourself?

Maybe your goal in life is to be of service to others. If you don't take care of yourself, you'll have little to give to anyone else! If you allow yourself to be diminished by self-denial, inhibition of self-expression, and a non-assertive style, you'll gradually lose your effectiveness in helping others as well. Recall that the commandment is to "Love others *as you love yourself.*" How well do you you love yourself? Remember the "Behavioral Model for Personal Growth" in the last chapter? Read it over again now, and consider how you can love yourself better.

Your attitude toward yourself and your behavior are always in a cycle. When you are down on yourself, you will tend to act in self-denying ways. Others will see those actions and respond accordingly — as if you don't deserve much respect. When you see the way they treat you, it confirms your attitude: "I *knew* I wasn't worth a damn! Look how people treat me!"

Assertiveness training breaks up the cycle by teaching you — and "authorizing" you — to behave assertively. Since you won't do it for yourself, maybe you'll do it when someone else tells you to! The trainer says, "Never mind how strange it feels, go ahead and try this new approach." When you do try it, the result is more positive feedback from other people, which in turn improves your attitude about yourself.

This enhanced sense of self-worth is the beginning of a positive turn in the attitude-behavior-feedback-attitude cycle. You can achieve the same results on your own — or perhaps with some help over the rough spots — by following the procedures described in this book. We'll get into the details of a program for behavior change a couple of chapters down the road; for now, let's take a deeper look at this business of thoughts and attitudes.

Thoughts Which Get In The Way of Self-Assertion

There are some patterns of thinking — both nonassertive and aggressive — which are common obstacles to assertiveness. If you're like most folks, you've heard yourself saying things like these — at least once in a while:

> *I'm a failure.*
> *The world is treating me badly.*
> *I'm a helpless victim of circumstances.*
> *Nobody loves me.*
> *Everybody is judging me.*
> *Other people are in control of my destiny.*

Or, on the other side:

> *When I speak, people listen (or else!).*
> *The world owes me obedience.*
> *I don't need help from anybody.*
> *I'm not going to let them get away with that!*
> *People are no damn good.*

All of these ideas are false. (A few of them may, on occasion, be partly true in your life: you — and everybody else — will fail sometimes. And the world does sometimes treat us badly. And some of us are self-sufficient some of the time.)

The big problem with this kind of thinking is that you may begin to believe it. Distorted views of what's happening in your life may result from a number of circumstances. Sometimes bad events occur coincidentally and create an impression that life has it in for you. That idea can stick in your head and become a "self-fulfilling prophecy."

Most of us don't experience life as a devastating series of downers, but we all have days (and weeks!) which can bring us down on ourselves — at least for a while. Cognitive psychiatrist Aaron Beck has outlined some of the steps which commonly occur:

> • *a predisposition to think poorly of yourself.* Maybe

you've been out of a job for a while, or did poorly in school, or broke up a romance. Or perhaps you have a rather low self-concept. In any case, you are prepared to assume that whatever goes wrong, you're to blame.

• *a tendency to exaggerate problems.* Minor emergencies often seem catastrophic at the time. In the total scheme of things, however, most life situations are less critical than we assume.

• *an egocentric view of life events.* "Everything happens to me!" is the theme of this step. An objective view would tell a different story, but the victim sees everything that goes awry to be aimed at him or her.

• *a belief that life is either one way or the other.* This notion of good-bad, black-white, yes-no, limits your choices markedly. The fact is that there are a number of alternatives in most life situations.

• *a view of oneself as helpless or vulnerable.* How can I possibly do anything about all the problems in my life? You can begin to deal with them effectively if you'll break them down into small enough increments.

Helpful Aids for Handling Thoughts

A number of excellent "cognitive-behavioral" methods have been developed for dealing with your thinking patterns. Three of the most effective are stress inoculation, thought-stopping, and positive self-statements.

Stress Inoculation: This type of "inoculation" not only minimizes expected stress, it can also be used on the spot to deal with stress. (Canadian psychologist Donald Meichenbaum gets credit for this one.)

Assume you have a situation coming up which you know will be stressful, such as a job performance interview. Your supervisor tends to be a fast talker and not a good listener. In the past, you have become very uptight and upset.

To inoculate yourself this time, start by writing yourself a message about the situation beforehand. Speak to yourself as a wise counselor would. Here is a sample message:

"When you have your performance evaluation, relax. Don't let yourself be thrown off. It does no good to get upset. Remember your supervisor's style, and be ready for it. When your supervisor says something you question, be firm but polite in asking about it. Ask for time to consider further. Speak up about information the supervisor is forgetting. Be ready to list your accomplishments. You can handle this. Take a deep breath once in a while. You'll be fine. If surprises come, just roll with them. This is only one small event in your total life."

Once you have a tailor-made message, read it aloud several times before the actual situation arises. Read it especially when you start worrying excessively or when you feel undue anxiety.

Remember the essence of the message so you can repeat key portions silently during the actual event (e.g., interview). If you find yourself slipping back in confidence, listen within yourself for the key parts.

One of our clients used this method successfully with her estranged husband. They were to meet in court and Carolyn knew she would fall apart and perhaps ruin her chances for a fair settlement. She developed a stress inoculation message and practiced it often. When she entered the courtroom, her husband came up and said "Hi," and Carolyn immediately broke into tears and ran to the bathroom! While there, she re-read her message aloud several times, regained her confidence and "sailed through" both talking to him again and the subsequent proceedings. Afterwards, she was amazed that it worked! In the past, she would have continued to be upset and cry. Stress inoculation helped Carolyn through a very emotional event.

Thought Stopping: Have you ever had an annoying tune or thought continually "run through your head?" Nothing you do seems to work to stop it. That's the time to try "thought stopping," another method developed by psychiatrist Joseph Wolpe. Close your eyes right now and conjure up some recurring thought that bothers you. When it comes in clearly, yell "STOP!" out loud. (Make sure no one is nearby or they may think you a bit bizarre!) Your thoughts *will* actually stop. When they do, shift immediately to a pleasant thought to replace the unwanted one. The unwanted thought will typically return in short order, but if you will persistently repeat the procedure, it will be longer and longer before the offender sneaks back in. Soon, the unwanted thought will give up. No, you don't have to run around yelling "STOP!" continually! The technique works just as effectively when done silently in your head. Of course, you may still want to yell it out loud once in a while because it is so much fun!

One warning: Be careful that the unwanted thoughts are not actually carrying constructive messages that you're not catching on to. You need to pay attention to *some* unpleasant thoughts and act upon them! With practice and trial and error, however, the difference between good and not-so-good thoughts will become apparent.

Positive Self-Statements: "The hardest step for most people I know," commented high school counselor Gail Wainwright at an AT group meeting, "is to *be assertive with yourself:* to convince yourself to go ahead and take the action you know is needed!"

If your thoughts are filled with self-denying "rules" and "attitudes," your behavior will in all likelihood be similar. You may think in negative statements: "I'm not important." "My opinions don't count." "No one will be interested in what I have to say." "I'll probably make a fool of myself if I say anything." "I'm really not sure." "I have no right to say that." If so, chances are very good you will act accordingly — that is, you'll keep quiet and let others control the situation!

Try, for a short period of time, to allow yourself to say the *positive* form of those statements: "I am important." "My opinions count." "Someone will be interested in what I have to say." "I have a right to say that." You needn't *act* on any of these at this point, just get the feel of saying positive things to yourself. The positive self-statements procedure simply consists of developing complimentary statements about yourself that you memorize and repeat regularly. The purpose is to build self-confidence. Examples:

I am respected and admired by my friends.
I am a kind and loving person.
I have a job.
I handle anger well.
I got through school successfully.
I am firm when the situation calls for it.

Some of the statements you choose may not be totally true of you, but we want you to "fudge" a little at first. Then proceed as if they were true. Place these statements on the refrigerator, on the bathroom wall, in your purse or wallet. Regularly remind youself that you are a positive and valuable person.

Positive self-statements can be used as replacement thoughts in conjunction with thought stopping. Or, they can be part of your stress inoculation message.

After you have practiced the positive thoughts for a while, you may wish to begin — still in your own thoughts — to consider the ways you would act in those situations if you followed through on the thoughts. Perhaps, for example, you were thinking, "Someone will be interested in what I have to say," in regard to joining in on a group discussion. If you were to imagine *acting* on that thought, you might see yourself asking a question of one of the more outspoken participants. Or, maybe you could just start out by saying, "I agree."

Think about ways you could *act* like a person who *thinks* positively!

Stop Imagining the Worst!

Too often people do not respond assertively because they have conjured up dire consequences: "If I do this, she'll be mad"; "I could never say that because he'd fire me"; "I'll feel guilty"; "She'll divorce me"; "My mother always cries"; "I'd hurt him too much." On and on go the imagined disasters. A part of the mind seems to work overtime to stifle self-expression.

Psychologist Albert Ellis calls this "catastrophisizing," and he has done a remarkable job of pointing out how such irrational beliefs hurt our chances of handling life situations well. In *A New Guide To Rational Living,* Ellis and Robert Harper suggest that our thoughts always come before our emotional reactions to situations. Ellis and Harper describe some of the irrational ideas and beliefs about how life "ought to be" that lead to upsetting emotions, thus blocking adequate responses. These beliefs relate to such life events as rejection, fear, being treated unfairly. Read Ellis and Harper's book, and stop inhibiting your assertiveness by believing (irrationally) that the world should somehow be perfect!

"What Else Can I Do About My Thoughts?"

UCLA psychologist Gary Emery is another highly regarded specialist in the cognitive therapy procedures. He has described a number of effective strategies and techniques for those who wish to make changes in their thinking patterns and "internal conversations."

You may find one or several of the procedures of help:

• *get to know and be aware of yourself.* A continuing quest for greater self awareness — your goals, dreams, feelings, attitudes, beliefs, limitations, problems — will give you a solid foundation for your self-improvement efforts.

• *recognize and keep track of your "automatic thoughts."* This term is used to describe the involuntary inner

dialogue you experience when you face a stressful situation
(e.g. "Oh dear, this is going to be...").

• *ask yourself questions to clarify your reactions to an
event.* Is there good evidence for your assumptions? How
logical is your reaction? Could you be oversimplifying things?
Exaggerating? Taking the situation out of context?

• *consider possible alternative explanations.* Look at the
situation from another viewpoint. Modify one fact at a time
and see what happens.

• *ask yourself, "So what?"* Does it really matter? Even if
the situation is actually as bad as you suspect, will the
consequences be lasting? Will anybody really be hurt?

• *try to substitute positive images.* See if you can come
up with a "silver lining." Might the bad news contain (or
hide) some *good* news?

• *identify the payoffs for you.* Are you getting some
reward for feeling bad? More attention, perhaps? Special
help? Excused from work or school? Might there be an even
better payoff for changing your outlook?

• *what if it really does happen?* What's the worst
outcome likely to bring? Can you act for a while as if the
feared event had already happened? Is it really as bad as you
thought?

• *do some very specific "homework" to change your
thoughts.* Go back to the previous section and develop a plan
for positive self-statements, or stress inoculation, or thought
stopping. Write your plan in your log, then do your
homework!

Are Some More Equal Than Others?

One of our most important goals for this book is to help
you recognize that you are *equal* to others on a human level.
True, there will always be someone more talented, more
assertive, more beautiful, more powerful, more wealthy,
more educated.... But you are just as good, just as valuable,
just as important as anyone else *as a human being.* That's a

terribly important idea which you may wish to read more about; try the Constitition of the United States, or the United Nations *Universal Declaration of Human Rights,* or the *Bible,* or the *Koran,* or the writings of Confucius, or...

10

There's Nothing to Be Afraid Of

Courage is resistance to fear, mastery of fear — not absence of fear.

— Mark Twain

Many readers of *Your Perfect Right* — perhaps you, too — find *anxiety* to be the most significant obstacle to greater assertiveness. "Sure," you say, "I know *how* to express myself! I just get really uptight about doing it. The risks seem too great. I want people to like me...."

Perhaps you find yourself perspiring heavily, your heart racing, your hands icy, as you walk into a job interview. Or maybe you have avoided asking your boss for a raise because you fear the words will catch in your throat. Do you take the long way home so you don't have to confront the neighbor who is always asking favors which you're afraid to refuse? You may even be among the surprisingly large proportion of the population known as *agoraphobics*, whose fears of social contact are so pervasive that they elect to remain at home virtually all the time.

You may not even be aware of the source of such fears. Often, they result from childhood experiences — for example, well-meaning parents may have taught you to "speak only when spoken to."

Although learning to be assertive will help to reduce such fears, when the level of anxiety is very high it may be necessary to deal more directly with the anxiety itself. To overcome fear, nervousness, anxiety and stress about assertiveness, it is necessary to determine what *causes* the reaction. Once you know what you are dealing with, you can learn methods to eliminate the fear.

We suggest you begin by *tracing* your fear. Narrow down exactly what causes you to feel afraid in the process of assertiveness. Use your log to record your reactions sysematically. Learn to keep track of what is causing your anxiety level to rise. The following section will help you to be more effective in learning about your anxiety.

Finding Your Fears: The SUD Scale

A useful aid in assessing your own anxiety level is the "SUD scale." "SUD" is an acronym for Subjective Units of Disturbance — simply a way of rating your own physical feelings of anxiety on a scale of 0-100. Because anxiety has physical elements, you can become aware of your degree of discomfort in a situation by "tuning in" to your body's indicators: heart rate (pulse), breathing rate, coldness in hands and feet, perspiration (particularly in hands), and muscle tension. (There are others, but most of us usually are not aware of them. Biofeedback training is sometimes used to allow people to learn when they are relaxed or anxious, since it offers an automatic monitor of physical indicators.)

Try this: get yourself as relaxed as you can right now — lie flat on the couch or floor or relax in your chair, breathe deeply, relax all the muscles in your body, and imagine a very relaxing scene (lying on the beach, floating on a cloud). Allow yourself to relax in this way for at least five minutes, paying attention to your heartbeat, breathing, hand temperature and dryness, muscle relaxation. Those relaxed feelings can be given a SUD scale value of 0, to represent near-total relaxation. If you did not do the relaxation exercise, but are reading this alone, relatively quietly and comfortably, you may consider yourself somewhere around 20 on the SUD scale.

At the opposite end of the scale, visualize the most frightening scene you can imagine. With your eyes closed, picture yourself narrowly escaping an accident, or being near the center of an earthquake or flood. Pay attention to the same body signals: heart rate/pulse, breathing, hand temperature/moisture, muscle relaxation. These fearful feelings can be given a SUD scale value of 100 — almost totally anxious.

Now you have a roughly calibrated comfort/discomfort scale which you can use to help yourself evaluate just how anxious you are in any given situation. Each 10 points on the scale represents a "just noticeable difference" up or down from the units above and below. Thus, 70 is slightly more anxious than 60, and by the same amount more comfortable than 80. (The SUD scale is too subjective to be able to define more closely than 10 units.)

Most of us function normally in the range of 20-50 SUDs. A few life situations will raise anxiety above 50 for short periods, and on rare occasions (rare for most of us, anyway!) one can relax below 20.

The SUD scale can help you to identify those life situations which are most troublesome. Once again, being systematic in your observations of yourself can pay big dividends! The procedure described below shows a way to use the SUD scale to develop a "plan of attack" against your fears.

List/Group/Label

A method developed by Patsy Tanabe-Endsley in the

field of creative writing will be helpful. In her book, *Project Write*, she tells how to list, group, and label ideas. We can use her system by substituting "fears or anxieties" for "ideas."

Start by recording or *listing* life situations when you feel fear or anxiety. Use some space in your log to list all your reactions that hinder your assertiveness, including the situation or event involved, people, circumstances, other factors which contributed to your reaction. Assign a SUDS value, as described in the previous section, to each of the items on your list.

Next, find the reactions on your list which are similar, those that seem to have a common theme, and *group* them together. Now see if you can *label* your groups, applying appropriate names to each grouping of anxiety-producing factors. Among your groups may be such common phobias as fears of snakes or spiders or heights or enclosed places. Interpersonal fears are more likely to be the problem in assertiveness. Fears of criticism, rejection, anger or aggression, or hurting the feelings of others greatly hinder your assertive response.

You may find a grouping which centers around one or more of the situations given in the Assertiveness Inventory in Chapter 7. Instead of a classic fear like rejection, you may simply experience a good deal of anxiety when standing in line or when facing salespersons. Perhaps people in authority scare you. Obviously, your assertiveness will not be optimum if your anxiety is already working against you beforehand!

Now, one more step in this analysis of your fears. In each labeled group, relist the items in order, according to the SUDS scores you have assigned. Now you have a rough agenda, in priority order, for dealing with your anxieties! Usually it is best to start working to reduce or overcome those which are most disturbing before you attempt to develop your assertive skills further.

The sample log page will help make this process clearer.

March 23, 1988

Today I'm going to write down situations when I feel anxious, including a "SUDS" estimate. I want to try the "list, group, label" method to see if I can figure out any patterns of fears.

1. Magazine article about open-heart surgery made me nauseous.   *SUDS 50*

2. I was upset when Jose ignored me at lunch.   *SUDS 30*

3. The boss looked disgusted when I made several mistakes at work.   *SUDS 65*

4. Elise told me she talked with Connie [ex-wife] about the kids. I was so angry that Connie criticized my discipline.
          SUDS 80!

5. Roommate didn't help with the dishes.   *SUDS 55*

6. Cut my finger; seeing the blood made me queasy. SUDS 35

7. I was embarrassed about being late to the meeting. SUDS 25

8. Friends teased me about my new haircut.   *SUDS 25*

Groups:	*Labels:*
A. 2, 3, 7, 8	*Being too sensitive*
B. 4, 5	*Anger*
C. 1, 6	*Medical fears*

Well, if this is a typical day, looks like I'm more sensitive about criticism than I thought. Maybe I should look into that "desensitization" exercise Dr. G told me about.

Overcoming Anxiety

Now that you have carefully identified the anxieties which are inhibiting your assertiveness, you will want to begin a program to overcome them. There are a number of effective approaches. Since this topic is a book in itself, let us briefly describe one popular approach, and then refer you to other resources for further information.

An assertiveness training pioneer, Philadelphia psychiatrist Joseph Wolpe, developed an immeasurably valuable procedure for dealing with anxiety called *systematic desensitization*. Like AT, systematic desensitization is based on learning principles; you *learned* to be anxious about expressing yourself, and you can *unlearn* it. No one was born fearful!

Practically speaking, it is not possible to be relaxed and anxious at the same time. The process of desensitization involves repeated association of an anxiety-producing situation with a feeling of deep relaxation throughout your body. Gradually, you learn to "automatically" associate relaxation, instead of anxiety, with the situation. In a therapeutic desensitization, the client first learns to relax the entire body completely through practicing a series of deep muscle relaxation exercises, or through hypnosis. The anxious situation is then presented in a series of imagined scenes, arranged in a hierarchy from least to greatest anxiety.

Here's how it works: Assume you are afraid of heights. Climbing a ladder would be an appropriate fear stimulus; your hierarchy probably lists increased anxiety with each higher rung. Your first session involves learning to relax fully. A relaxing scene, such as a warm day at the beach, floating on a cloud, or lying in a hammock, is visualized in detail during the relaxation exercise. You are instructed to practice relaxation over a period of several days.

In a later session, the therapist asks you to become fully relaxed, close your eyes and visualize your relaxing scene. You are then told to imagine yourself stepping onto the first rung of the ladder and to be aware of the anxiety which results. After five to fifteen seconds you'll switch your visualization back to your relaxing scene, relaxing once again. This procedure is repeated several times for each step of the ladder, and the repeated exposure to your anxious scene while you are relaxed gradually reduces your fear of the stimulus scenes.

The intricacies of the procedure are somewhat more complex, but that is the essence of desensitization. It has been proven effective for a wide range of fears, including phobic reactions to heights, public speaking, animals, flying, test taking, social contact, and many more.

If you are very concerned about your anxiety, you may wish to do some further reading. Two good books on the topic are *BT* (*Behavior Therapy*) by Spencer Rathus (1978) and *StressMap* by Michele Haney and Ed Boenisch (1982). Both books explore self-help procedures for anxiety and describe further resources available.

Expect to invest some time — probably several weeks — practicing the methods of anxiety relief described here and in the resources noted. It took time for you to learn to be anxious; it will take time to learn to overcome it.

This discussion of anxiety about assertiveness is not meant to discourage you. On the contrary, most readers will find themselves able to handle their mild discomfort about self-expression without major difficulty. There are some of us, however, who do need some extra help in overcoming obstacles. Don't be embarrassed or hesitant about asking for help, just as you would seek competent medical aid for a physical problem. Then, when you've cleared up the anxiety obstacle, turn back to the procedures outlined in this book for developing your assertiveness.

Summary

Feelings of nervousness, anxiety reactions, and fear are common when thinking about and acting assertively. Often, practicing assertive responses will reduce these uneasy reactions to manageable levels. Practice will make assertion feel more natural to you. If you feel that you are still too afraid, there are systematic ways to identify the situations which trigger fearful reactions, and to reduce the level of anxiety.

Simply understanding a fear is seldom powerful enough to reduce it significantly. Self-help methods which help eliminate or lower the fear to manageable levels are often successful. Professional therapy is recommended when your own efforts are not enough.

HOW ARE YOU DOING?

From time to time throughout *Your Perfect Right,* we've inserted this ''break'' in the text to get you to pause and take stock. No big formal deal — just a periodic checkup to help you stay on track.

Take some time now to answer the questions below. Be honest with yourself, and let the answers guide your next steps.

• Have you read and understood all the material in the previous chapters?
• Do our explanations and examples fit with your own experience?
  If not, can you adapt them to your needs?
• Are you doing the exercises and answering the questions we have raised?
• Has ''assertiveness'' begun to mean something real to you?
• Have you set some preliminary goals for your growth in assertiveness?
• Are you keeping a log of your progress?
• Have you asked for help if you need it for anxiety or other obstacles?
• Have you identified your own shortcomings in assertiveness: anxiety, attitudes, social skills?

11

Developing Assertive Behavior Skills

Peace cannot be kept by force. It can only be achieved by understanding.
— Albert Einstein

Perhaps you have heard it said that "when two engineers (lawyers, housekeepers, plumbers, nurses) are talking together and a psychologist walks up and joins the conversation, there are now two engineers and a psychologist, but when two psychologists are talking and an engineer (substitute your own favorite) walks up and joins them, there are now three psychologists!" Everyone believes she/he is a psychologist in some sense. Indeed, we all have some practical first-hand knowledge of human behavior, beginning with ourselves.

Changing Behavior and Attitudes

Popular wisdom often suggests that to improve yourself you need to "change your attitude." For many years, until quite recently, behavioral psychologists argued that it was more important to change *behavior*, that attitude change would follow.

A great deal of recent research in a field of psychology called *cognitive behavior therapy* has shown that, for many people at least, *thoughts are as important as actions* in bringing about life changes.

In the first three editions of this book, we advocated the position of traditional behavior therapy, that it was easier and more effective to change behavior first, then attitude change will slowly follow. While we still consider attitude change the "tougher nut to crack," we have learned that one's thinking processes can be modified by procedures such as those we described in Chapter 9, and that such changes will powerfully affect one's behavior.

Positive self-statements provide a good example. By consciously telling yourself "I have the ability to succeed in this situation," you greatly enhance your chances of success, even without any other changes. We view and interpret life events through our own unique attitudes and beliefs about ourselves and the world, and we act according to those interpretations. If I go about believing that "I am no damn good," I will approach life situations with an outlook of failure — and thus increase my chance of failure. If I tell myself I am capable of succeeding, my actions will be more likely to follow a pattern of success.

For a time, the "cognitive folks" seemed to have everyone convinced that such changed thinking was all-important. That usually happens when a new idea emerges from psychological research. Very recently, the "pendulum" has begun to swing back toward a more moderate position, and that is the view we hold: *Both thinking and behavior are vital elements in the process of bringing about personal growth.* Some people respond more readily to cognitive (thinking) interventions, others to behavioral (action) interventions. In any comprehensive program for growth, therefore, *both* areas must be dealt with. Put most of your energy into whichever is most helpful for *you*! (Funny how psychological research catches up with common sense, if we allow enough time to pass!)

As you begin the process of becoming more assertive, we won't ask you to wake up some morning and say, "Today, I'm a new, assertive person!" You will find here, spelled out in detail in the following chapter, a systematic, step-by-step guide to change. The key to developing assertiveness is *practice*.

Cycles of behavior tend to repeat, and to perpetuate themselves, until a decisive intervention occurs. People who have acted nonassertively or aggressively in relationships for a long time typically don't think much of themselves. Their behavior toward others may be inhibited or abusive — either usually is met with scorn, disdain, or avoidance. When those inevitable responses come, such a person says, "See, I knew I was no damn good!" The person is confirmed in a low self-evaluation, and the cycle is repeated: self-defeating behavior, negative feedback from others, self-critical attitude, self-defeating behavior, and so on....

The cycle can be reversed, becoming a positive sequence: more appropriately assertive behavior gains more positive responses from others; positive feedback leads to an improved evaluation of self-worth: ("Wow, people are treating me like a worthwhile person!"); and improved attitudes about oneself result in further assertiveness.

Or, the cycle may be entered at the point of thoughts: by saying positive things to yourself and beginning to think of yourself as a valuable person, you'll begin to act more appropriately. Your more effective action will usually produce more positive responses from others and the resulting confirmation of the original thought: "Maybe I *am* a good person, after all!"

Harold had been convinced for years that he was truly worthless. He was totally dependent upon his wife for emotional support and, despite a rather handsome appearance and ability to express himself well, had literally no friends. Imagine his utter despair when his wife left him! Fortunately, Harold was already in therapy at the time, and was willing to try to make contact with other people. When his first attempts at assertiveness with eligible women were successful, the reward of this response to his assertions was very great! Harold's entire outlook toward himself changed, and he became much more assertive in a variety of situations.

Not everyone, to be sure, will experience such an immediate "payoff" for assertion; and not all assertions are fully successful. Success usually requires a great deal of patience, and a gradual process of handling more and more difficult situations.

Generally we have found is that *assertiveness is self-rewarding*. It feels good to have others begin to respond more attentively, to achieve one's goals in relationships, to find situations going one's way more often. And you can make these changes happen.

Remember, begin with assertions where you are somewhat certain of success before proceeding to more difficult ones requiring greater confidence and skill. It is often quite helpful and reassuring to obtain support and guidance from a friend, practice partner, teacher, or professional therapist.

Keep in mind that changed behavior leads to changed attitudes about oneself and one's impact upon people and situations. Moreover, changed thinking leads to changed behavior. The following chapter presents the steps involved in bringing about these changes. Read all the material carefully first. Then begin to follow the steps in your own life. You'll like the difference in you!

When You Are Ready to Begin

First, make certain that you understand thoroughly the basic principles of assertion. Realizing the differences between assertive and aggressive behavior is important to your understanding and success. Re-read Chapters 2, 4, and 5 if you need to.

Second, decide whether you are ready to begin trying self-assertive behavior on your own. If you have chronic patterns of nonassertion or aggression *or* if you are highly anxious, be more cautious. We recommend slow and careful practice and work with another person, preferably a trained therapist, as a facilitator. This recommendation is particularly strong for those who feel *very* anxious about beginning, as we discussed in Chapter 10.

Third, your initial attempts at being assertive should be chosen for their high potential of success, so as to provide reinforcement. The more successfully you assert yourself at first, the more likely you are to be successful from then on!

Begin with small assertions that are likely to be rewarding, and from there proceed to more difficult assertions. Proceed with care when taking it upon your own initiative to attempt a difficult assertion without special preparation. And be especially careful not to instigate an assertion where you are likely to fail miserably, thus inhibiting further attempts at assertiveness.

If you do suffer a setback, which very well may happen, take time carefully to analyze the situation and regain your confidence, getting help from a friend or facilitator if necessary. Especially in the early stages of assertion, it is not unusual to experience difficulty due to inadequate technique or overzealousness to the point of aggression. Either could cause negative returns, particularly if the other individual becomes hostile and highly aggressive. Don't let such an occurrence stop you. Consider your goal again, and remember that although success requires practice, the rewards are great.

There will be some failures. These procedures will not turn you into a 100 percent success in all your relationships! There are no instant or magic answers to life's problems. Assertiveness does not always work — for *us* either! Sometimes, your goals will be incompatible with the other person's. Two people can't be at the head of the same line. (Letting the other person go first can be an assertive act, too!) At times, others may be unreasonable or unyielding, and the best of assertions will be to no avail.

Also, because you're human, you'll blow it sometimes —

as we all do. Allow yourself to make mistakes! You'll be uncomfortable, disappointed, discouraged. Reassess, practice, then try again.

If you feel your assertions are failing a bit too often, take a close look at what's going on. Are you setting your goals too high? Take small steps to ensure success! Are you overdoing it and becoming aggressive? Monitor your behavior carefully — refer to your log and check yourself. (Some aggression is to be expected at first. The pendulum will balance in a short time.)

We all want our assertions to work, and to achieve our goals. Nevertheless, the greatest value of self-assertion is the good feeling that comes from having expressed yourself. To know that you have a *perfect right* to self-expression, and to feel free to say what you're feeling are the best benefits of all.

Usually, you'll find assertiveness will make things happen. But whether it works or not, remember how good it felt to speak up for yourself! You did what you could, even if the outcome wasn't what you hoped for. If you have genuinely tried and done all you can, that's all you can ask of yourself!

One final caution: Nothing turns people off faster than a self-righteous attitude. Avoid the trap some new assertiveness trainees fall into — feeling you *must* assert yourself in all situations, at all costs. Let moderation, consideration for others, and common sense prevail! (More on this in Chapter 19.)

Ready to move ahead? Chapter 12 shows how — step by step.

12

One Step At a Time

*Believe in life! Always human beings will live
and progress to greater, broader, and fuller life.*
— W. E. B. DuBois

The Step-By-Step Process for Increasing Your Assertiveness

Step 1. Observe your own behavior. Are you asserting
yourself adequately? Are you satisfied with your effectiveness
in interpersonal relationships? Look over your personal log,
and the discussion in Chapters 1-6, and assess how you feel
about yourself and your behavior.

Step 2. Keep track of your assertiveness. Keep your log
very carefully for a week. Each day, record those situations in
which you found yourself responding assertively, those in
which you blew it, and those you avoided altogether so you
would not have to face the need to act assertively. Be honest
with yourself, and systematic, following the guidelines for
self-assessment described in Chapter 7.

Step 3. Set realistic goals for yourself. Your
self-assessment will help you select specific targets for your
growth in assertiveness. Pick out situations in which, or
people toward whom, you want to become more effective. Be
sure to start with a small, low-risk step to maximize your
chances of success. (See Chapter 8.)

Step 4. Concentrate on a particular situation. Spend a few moments with your eyes closed, imagining how you handled a specific incident (being short-changed at the supermarket, having a friend "talk your ear off" on the telephone when you had too much to do, letting the boss make you feel like "two cents" over a small mistake). Imagine vividly the actual details, including your specific feelings at the time and afterward. Appendix A offers many sample situations for your practice.

Step 5. Review your responses. Get out your log and write down your behavior in Step 4. Make use of the components of assertiveness noted in Chapter 6 (eye contact, body posture, gestures, facial expression, voice, message content, etc.) Look carefully at the components of your behavior in the recalled incident, including your thoughts. Note your strengths. Be aware of those components which represent nonassertive or aggressive behavior. If a major element of your response involves anxiety, refer to the discussion in Chapter 10. Do not attempt to force yourself into very painful situations. On the other hand, do not avoid new growth if it is only moderately uncomfortable!

Step 6. Observe an effective model. At this point it would be very helpful to watch someone who handles the same situation very well. Again, watch for the components discussed in Chapter 6, particularly the *style* — the words are less important. If the model is a friend, discuss his/her approach, and its consequences.

Step 7. Consider alternative responses. What are other possible ways the incident could be handled? Could you deal with it more directly? More firmly? Less offensively? Refer to the chart in Chapter 4, and differentiate among nonassertive, aggressive, and assertive responses.

Step 8. Imagine yourself handling the situation. Close your eyes and visualize yourself dealing effectively with your practice situation. You may act similarly to the model in Step 6, or in a very different way. Be assertive, but be as much your natural self as you can. Develop strategies or ways of coping with blocks in your visualization. If you notice yourself feeling anxious, calm yourself. If negative thoughts interrupt your assertion, replace them with positive statements. Self-correct as you proceed. Cope with disruptions of your assertive response in your visualization. Repeat this step as often as necessary until you can imagine yourself handling the situation well.

Step 9. Practice positive thoughts. Spend some time going over the material in Chapter 9. Develop a list of several brief positive statements about yourself which are related to this situation (e.g., "I've had job interviews before, and have done alright"). Practice saying those statements to yourself several times. Remember, this is not a "script" for what to say to someone else, it is a "prompter" for what to say to yourself.

Step 10. Get help if you need it. As we have noted before, the process of becoming more assertive may require you to stretch yourself considerably. If you feel unable on your own to deal with the situations you have visualized, seek help from a qualified professional (see Appendix C).

Step 11. Try it out. You have examined your own behavior, considered alternatives, observed a model of more adaptive action, and practiced some positive thoughts about yourself. You are now prepared to begin trying out for yourself new ways of dealing with the problem situation. A repeat of Steps 6, 7, 8 and 9 may be needed until you are ready to proceed. It is important to select an alternative, more effective way of behaving in the problem situation. You may wish to follow your model and enact the same approach. Such a choice is appropriate, but should reflect an awareness that you are a unique person. You may not find the model's approach one which you want to adopt for yourself.

After selecting a more effective alternative behavior, role-play the situation with a friend, practice partner, teacher, or therapist. Try to follow the new response pattern you have selected. As in Steps 2, 4, and 5, make careful observation of your behavior, using audio or videotape whenever possible. Don't worry about not having your goals absolutely clear. As you try out new behavioral skills, you'll become more aware of what you want in the situation.

Step 12. Get feedback. This step essentially repeats Step 5 with emphasis on the positive aspects of your behavior. Note particularly the strengths of your performance, and go to work on your weaker areas.

Step 13. Behavior shaping. Steps 8, 9, 11 and 12 should be repeated as often as necessary to "shape" your behavior — by this process of successive approximations of your goal — until you feel comfortable dealing effectively with the situation.

Step 14. The real test. You are now ready to give your new response pattern a real test. Up to this point your preparation has taken place in a relatively secure environment. Nevertheless, careful training and repeated practice have prepared you to react almost automatically. You should be ready to proceed with an actual trial. If you are unwilling to do so, further rehearsals or help may be needed. (Repeat steps 8-12). Moving from intention to action — being assertive with yourself — may be the most important step of all!

Step 15. Further training. Repeat the procedures that help you develop your desired behaviors for other specific situations which have given you trouble. Look over Chapter 5 and Appendix A for examples which may be helpful in planning your own program for change.

Step 16. Social reinforcement. As a final step in establishing an independent behavior pattern, it is very important that you understand the need for on-going support and rewards. In order to maintain your new assertive skills, set up a system of rewards in your own environment. For example, you now know the good feeling that comes from a successful assertion and you can rest assured that this good response will continue. Admiration from others will be another continuing positive response to your growth. Write down in your log a personal checklist of specific reinforcements which are unique to your own environment and relationships.

We have spelled out this step-by-step process in detail because we know it works. Although we emphasize the importance of systematic procedures, we recommend you take into account your own personal needs, objectives, and learning style. Create a learning environment which will help you grow in assertiveness. No one system is right for everyone.

A number of approaches to assertiveness training have proved valuable, and you may wish to explore materials noted in the Bibliography for other important contributions to AT practice.

There is, of course, no substitute for *active practice* of assertive thoughts and behavior in your own life, when you choose to, as a means of developing greater assertiveness and enjoying its rewards.

HOW ARE YOU DOING?

From time to time throughout *Your Perfect Right,* we've inserted this "break" in the text to get you to pause and take stock. No big formal deal — just a periodic checkup to help you stay on track.

Take some time now to answer the questions below. Be honest with yourself, and let the answers guide your next steps.

• Have you read and understood all the material in the previous chapters?
• Do our explanations and examples fit with your own experience?
  If not, can you adapt them to your needs?
• Are you doing the exercises and answering the questions we have raised?
• Has "assertiveness" begun to mean something real to you?
• Have you set some preliminary goals for your growth in assertiveness?
• Are you keeping a log of your progress?
• Have you asked for help if you need it for anxiety or other obstacles?
• Have you identified your own shortcomings in assertiveness: anxiety, attitudes, social skills?

13

Assertiveness Builds
Equal Relationships

Unity is plural and, at minimum, is two.
— R. Buckminster Fuller

"Stand up for yourself" is the slogan often equated with being assertive. The first edition of *Your Perfect Right* was devoted almost exclusively to fostering that type of behavior. In a critical review of that first edition, published in the professional journal *Behavior Therapy*, the late psychiatrist Michael Serber noted our oversight. Serber, a colleague who had substantial influence on our work, wrote in that early review (1971):

Certainly, behavioral skills necessary to stand up to the multiple personal, social, and business situations confronting the majority of people are imperative to master. But what of other just as necessary skills, such as being able to give and take tenderness and affection? Is not the expression of affection toward other people also assertion? ...the ability to express warmth and affection, to be able to give and take feelings, including anger, badly needs...special attention...humanistic goals and behavioral techniques can yield both meaningful and concrete new behaviors.

We have observed that positive, caring feelings are more difficult for many people to express than "standing up for yourself" behavior. Expressions of warmth are often held back, particularly by adults. Embarrassment, fear of rejection or ridicule, the idea that reason is superior to emotion — all are excuses for not expressing warmth, caring, and love spontaneously.

Even "thank you" is difficult for some people. Geoffrey was president of a multimillion dollar giant organization, and was noted for rarely expressing appreciation to the people on his staff. A job well done was seldom openly rewarded, recognized, or even acknowledged. Because the chief executive was afraid to act in warm and positive ways (perhaps he might appear "soft," or others might come to *expect* rewards?), the morale of staff members in that organization was not very high.

To be a caring person, and to express that openly, seems to be a "high-risk" style in our society. How sad for all of us that we make it so difficult for warmth to be expressed openly! Assertiveness training can contribute much to greater freedom in communication of positive feelings toward others.

"What the World Needs Now..."

Thirty years ago, psychoanalyst Eric Fromm defined five types of love in his excellent book *The Art of Loving*. The book is old, but the concepts are timeless: fraternal love, maternal love, erotic love, love of God, and self-love.

Today's popular spokesperson for "love" is Leo Buscaglia, an educational psychologist and former faculty member of the University of Southern California. Buscaglia has folks thinking and talking about love as popular culture. Whether his influence will be as lasting as that of Fromm remains to be seen. Nevertheless, it is healthy for a society to be talking openly about love — particularly when so much of our attention is also devoted to war, crime, and violence.

Fraternal love — caring for other members of the human

family — is a very different quality than the popular romantic idea of "love." It is a vital and critically important aspect of our lives on this small planet. However independent we may become, we humans are fundamentally interdependent and social creatures!

Effective assertive communication can build positive, equal relationships between people — the most valuable assets any human being can have.

Some folks don't agree with us, of course. They identify assertiveness training with the "me decade" of the 1970s, when some AT was presented by careless, poorly trained, and sometimes downright unethical trainers as if its major purpose were to help get your way in life: "Oh yeah, that's where you learn to push other people around, isn't it?" Some popular books associated with assertiveness also taught a manipulative, "me first" style, unfortunately.

That is emphatically *not* what genuine assertiveness is about. We believe the world is too small, and human relationships too vital, for that kind of thinking. We hope you'll agree, and apply your assertive skills to building healthy, equal, loving relationships.

Reaching Out

Expressing your warm feelings for another person is a highly assertive act. And, as with other assertions we have noted, the action itself is more important by far than the words you use. This is even more true for expressions of caring. Nothing represents a more personal, individual expression than that which says, "You mean a great deal to me at this moment."

Here are some ways of communicating that message:
- A warm, firm, and extended handshake.
- A hug, the squeeze of an arm, an arm around the shoulders, an affectionate pat on the back, the squeeze of a hand held affectionately.
- Sincerely warm words, such as

> *"Thank you."*
> *"You're great!"*
> *"I really understand what you mean."*
> *"I like what you did."*
> *"I'm here."*
> *"I believe you."*
> *"I trust you"* (*better yet an* act *of trust*).
> *"I love you."*
> *"I believe in you."*
> *"I'm glad to see you."*
> *"You've been on my mind."*

- A warm smile.
- Extended eye contact.
- A gift of love (made by the giver, or uniquely special to the recipient).

None of these messages is new to you. Yet you may find it difficult to allow yourself to do or say them. It is too easy to be hung up on embarrassment, or to assume: "She knows how I feel," or "He doesn't care to hear that." But *who* doesn't care to hear that? All of us need to know we are cared about and admired and needed. If those around us are too subtle in their expressions of positive regard, we can too easily begin to doubt, and perhaps look elsewhere for human warmth.

In very intimate relationships — between lovers for example — it is often assumed that each partner knows the feelings of the other. Such assumptions may lead to the marriage counselor's office with complaints such as, "I never know how he feels," "She never tells me she loves me," "We just don't communicate any more." Frequently it is necessary to re-establish a communication pattern in which each partner expresses feelings openly — particularly those of caring. The expression of caring won't solve all the ills of an ailing marriage, but it can "shore up the foundation" by helping each partner remember what was good about the relationship in the first place!

We asked a group of university students to tell what makes each of them feel especially good. Some of their favorite experiences are in the following list (notice how many involve someone else caring!):

Acceptance of an invitation
Achievement
Affection
Approval
Assurance
Compliments from the opposite sex
Encouragement
Expressed interest of another
Friendliness
Getting an A on an exam
Giving a compliment
Good grades
Greeting someone else
Having a friend
Having someone say "hello"
Helping others
Implementation of ideas
Independence
Jobs completed
Keeping my plants alive
Laughter
Making new friends
My boyfriend's/girlfriend's actions of love toward me
Personal satisfaction with myself
Positive comment
Praise
Receiving a compliment
Recognition
Recognition when speaking
Request to repeat a job previously done
Satisfaction
Security

Singing
Spoken affirmation
Touch

We all need positive contacts with others. Therapists encounter many, many clients who are unhappy precisely because they are not getting such "strokes" in their lives.

Imagine the following scenes:

...While you are wandering alone at a large gathering, a stranger walks up to you and starts a conversation, and you no longer feel anxious and lost.

...Three days after you arrive in a new neighborhood, the couple next door come to welcome you with a pot of coffee and a freshly baked cake.

...During your visit in another country, you are looking in vain for a street sign. A native appears and asks, "May I help you find something?"

Take a few moments to jot down in your log how you would feel in each of those situations.

Thoughtful acts like these are not only strokes for the receiver, they produce warm feelings for the person who reached out assertively. People often hesitate to initiate contact in these ways for fear of rejection — a common response for avoiding assertions! Such initiative involves concern for the other person, and some courage of your own. Yet, realistically, who could reject such a kindness?

Often actions like these are easier than you might suppose. As you enter a classroom, meeting, bus, airplane, think how easy it would be to simply approach a vacant seat and ask the person sitting nearest, "Is anyone sitting there?" Not only have you found a place to sit — assuming the seat is available — *you have begun a conversation!* Having thus opened contact, you may easily proceed to find out more about the other person: "Where are you headed?" "Have you heard this lecturer before?" "My name is...."

Don't wait for others to take the initiative. Take the risk

of reaching out! It's a key means of caring about yourself and about others, and an important step toward greater assertiveness and more fun!.

"Thanks, I Needed That!"

Compliments are a frequent source of discomfort, sadly enough. To praise someone as a person or to recognize something someone has done may be a difficult thing for you. Again, we encourage practice. Go out of your way to praise others — not dishonestly or insincerely — but whenever a genuine opportunity presents itself. Don't concern yourself with waiting for the right words either. Your thoughtfulness — the honest expression of what you are feeling — will convey itself, *if you act!* Try simply, "I like what you did" or "Great!" or a big smile.

Accepting compliments — receiving very supportive statements directed toward you, or about you to a third person — is perhaps an even more challenging task, particularly difficult if you are not feeling good about yourself. Nevertheless, it is an assertive act — and mutually enhancing — to accept praise from another person.

Think about it: you really have no right to deny another person's *perception* of you. If you say, "Oh, you just caught me on a good day!" or "It wasn't anything special" or "It was an accident that it turned out well," you have in effect said the complimentor has poor judgment. It is as if you told that person, "You're wrong!" Try to allow everyone the right to feelings, and if they are positive toward you, do others — and yourself — the courtesy of accepting.

You don't have to go around praising yourself, or taking credit for achievements which are not your own. However, when another person sincerely wishes to convey a positive comment about you, *allow* the expression, without rejection or qualification. Try saying at the least, "It's hard for me to accept that, but thank you," or better yet simply, "That feels good" or "I like to hear that."

Friendship

"Nancy has seen me at my worst, watched me make stupid mistakes, felt the sting of my unjustified anger, and been there when I was coming apart at the seams. It's amazing; she's still my friend!"

There is no relationship quite like that of friendship. Not so irrational as love, yet far more intense than acquaintance, friendship is perhaps the least understood of human interactions.

Actual *knowledge* about friendship continues to be sketchy at best; most relationship research involves strangers or lovers. Yet some popular wisdom is useful in examining the bond between friends:

...Friends have some interests in common.

...Friends share an on-going relationship, with periodic (although not necessarily regular) contact.

...Friends trust one another, at least to some extent, with information, money, safety, other relationships.

...Friends can say "no" to each other and still remain friends.

...Friends can see — and accept — the worst in each other.

...Friends rarely feel they "owe" each other anything; give and take is without obligation between them (perhaps with some limits!).

...Friendship is also characterized by understanding, communication, acceptance, lack of embarrassment, trust.

Friendship is held within us, an attitude toward another person much like love, anger, or prejudice. It requires no regular outward expression. It requires merely a *feeling of commitment* to the relationship. Often such a feeling is supported by the belief that the other person cares about you, that the other values the relationship as well. If we believe that we are important to each other — important enough that we think of each other warmly now and again — we will likely remain friends, even if we don't see each other for years.

It is common to see tearful reunions at airports, parties and homecomings between friends who have not seen each other for years. Friendships often survive no more contact than an annual ritual holiday card! What keeps them going? Can such a relationship really be called a "friendship?" Why not?

But what has this to do with assertiveness? How does assertive action contribute to friendship, or vice versa?

Let us pose an unproven theory for your consideration: *If you act assertively most of the time, you are more likely to have satisfying relationships than if you act in nonassertive or aggressive ways.* We cannot prove that idea. In fact, we have not even dreamed up a research study which would allow us to test it (if you do, we would love to hear from you!). But our observation of assertive people over many years leads us to conclude that it is a pretty good bet!

Acting on that hypothesis, then, and assuming that you would like to have satisfying relationships, we invite you to apply the assertive skills you are learning to the development of friendship:

...Take the risks necessary to build an acquaintance into a friend.

...Allow yourself to be seen as you are by your friend.

...Share something of yourself you would not ordinarily tell someone else.

...Be spontaneous with your new friend, suggest an activity on the spur of the moment, really listen to what is important in your friend's life, give a gift for no special occasion.

...Ask your friend's advice with a problem or help with a project (remembering that an assertive friend can say "no" and still like you!)

...Simply tell the person you like him/her.

...Clear the air between you; if you are annoyed or suspect that your friend may be, bring it up.

...Get *honest*. Don't allow assumptions to define your relationship. If the relationship can't handle it, it probably would not have lasted anyway; if it can, you'll be miles ahead!

As adults, friendship helps to define who we are, much as family does when we are children. (The absence of friends also says a great deal about us.) Assertive action on your part can make all the difference in nurturing friendships. Maybe you've put it off long enough?

Parents and Children in the Assertive Family

How long has it been since you were on a seesaw or teeter-totter? Remember how you could affect the ride of the person on the other end by shifting your weight forward or back? If you moved forward quickly, your friend would likely drop with a solid bump! By leaning way back, you could keep the other suspended in mid-air.

Families and other interpersonal systems have a balance system not unlike that of the seesaw. A change in one member of the family will generally upset the balance of the total system, affecting everyone. Often families are strong "resistors" of change because of the delicate balance in family relationships, even though the system may be painful or even destructive.

Becoming more assertive is clearly a change which may upset the family balance.

Ellen, for example, had been a passive wife and mother for years. As she began to express a new assertiveness, severe strains were introduced into the family system. The children, previously able to manipulate her easily, had to find new and more direct avenues to achieve their goals. Reluctantly supportive, husband Joe was soon ironing his own shirts and sharing in household chores, since Ellen had gone back to school full time.

Such changes present a difficult adjustment for everyone. The prospect of such disruption of the family balance can be a considerable obstacle to the person who wishes to become more assertive. A traditional partner may actively resist changes which demand a greater share of responsibility for the family's well-being. For the children, a whole new set of challenges is introduced, as they learn to deal with the requirements of increased self-reliance.

Out of the Mouths of Babes...

It has been said that "the last frontier of human rights is that of the rights of children." Despite the history of apparent dedication to individual rights in the United States, and even despite the recent gains in rights for minorities, women, and others who have been denied and oppressed, we have made few changes in our basic notions that children are second-class citizens. The glorification of "youth" in popular media, dress styles, music, and literature has not carried over into a comparable respect for the rights of those who are young.

Without debating the relative concerns of innocence and inexperience vs. age and wisdom, let us simply suggest that assertive children, like assertive adults, are likely to be healthier and happier, more honest, and less manipulative. Feeling better about themselves, these youngsters are headed toward more self-actualized adulthood.

We favor a conscious effort in families, schools, churches, and public agencies to foster assertiveness in young people. Let's create conditions which will tolerate — even support — their natural spontaneity, honesty and openness, rather than sacrificing it to parent anxiety and school authority.

Let us be clear — we do not advocate totally permissive child-rearing. The real world places limits upon us all, and children need to learn that fact early if they are to develop adequate life s-u-r-v-i-v-a-l skills. However, we consider it vital that families, schools, and other child rearing social systems view children as human beings worthy of respect,

honor their basic human rights, value their honest
self-expression, and teach them the skills to act accordingly.

Assertive skills are valuable for children in dealing with
their peers, teachers, siblings and parents. Mike Emmons
recently led two assertiveness groups (grades 1-3 and 4-6) at a
local elementary school. The youngsters got enthusiastically
involved, and volunteered a few situations from their daily
experience:

> *What do you do if someone pushes in front of you in
> lunch line?*
>
> *My sister borrows my things without asking. What
> should I say?*
>
> *When it's Joe's turn to be "out" in handball, he won't
> leave.*
>
> *What do you do if someone teases you or calls you
> names?*
>
> *The woman I babysit for forgot to pay me. I told my
> Mom, but she said I should call her. I am too
> embarrassed.*

The children easily understood the meaning of
assertiveness. They practiced the skills, and especially
enjoyed being videotaped in the process. Even the children's
performance feedback to each other was specific and helpful.
Children can learn the basics of assertiveness and apply them
to situations in their own lives.

Parents often have difficulty discriminating between
assertion and aggression when disciplining or dealing firmly
with their youngsters. The definition of assertiveness applies
to parent-child relationships! Although each situation is
unique, the key to defining assertiveness in family
interactions is *mutual respect*. Children, like parents, are
individual human beings. They deserve fair treatment, and
non-aggressive discipline.

Most of the principles and procedures advocated
elsewhere in this book apply to the development of
assertiveness in children. We won't present any specialized

material here. Interested readers may wish to consult the books *Liking Myself*, and *The Mouse, the Monster, and Me*, written directly for younger children by Denver psychologist Pat Palmer.

They Do Grow Up, Don't They?

Independence from our parents may be the single most important life issue we all face, certainly it is the core around which growing up revolves. Some rebelliousness is normal and healthy for teenagers, and facilitates their developing independence. Parental dominance and teenage inhibition may slow down that process, and delay the necessary steps toward independent adulthood.

Unresolved ties with parents sometimes restrict independence in the lives of adults of all ages. In our experience, an assertive approach by the "child" can clear the air, make the situation clear to the parent, and allow needed expression of feelings on both sides.

Such a confrontation is almost inevitably painful, and it is a considerable risk for both parent and child to open up old wounds. Despite this obstacle, we believe continued silence exacts much too high a price. Adults who avoid dealing with their parents or adult children as they would any other adult with whom they feel a special closeness can suffer unmeasured guilt, self-denial, inhibition, repressed anger, and often depression.

New York psychologists Janet Wolfe and Iris Fodor have done excellent work with the relationship of adult mothers and daughters, and their five steps toward a new assertive mother-daughter relationship are useful for anyone who is dealing with this issue:

...Recognize the life cycle issues each party is dealing with (eg. economic independence, menopause, retirement, etc.)

...Identify attitudes or beliefs which inhibit assertive communication (eg. "Don't talk back to your father.")

...Figure out the rights and goals of each party.

...Identify emotions (eg. anxiety, guilt) which interfere with pursuing goals.

...Try out new forms of relationship (eg. adult-to-adult, rather than parent-to-child).

Summary

To sum up this discussion of assertiveness in the family:

• Assertive behavior enhances both individuals and relationships.

• Honest, open and nonhurtful assertive communication is desirable and highly valuable in families.

• Children as well as adults should learn to be assertive within the family and beyond it.

• The principles and procedures for defining and learning assertiveness, which are described in this book, are applicable to adults and to children (i.e., modelling, rehearsal, feedback, practice, reinforcement, mutual respect, and individual rights).

Change in family systems is more difficult, more time and energy consuming, and potentially more risky (families can and do break up) than is change in individual behavior. We encourage you to evaluate carefully, to proceed slowly, to involve everyone openly, to avoid coercion, to tolerate failure, and to remember that nobody and no approach is perfect! Notwithstanding these cautions, we also encourage you to work toward the development of an "assertive family." It can be a tremendously exciting and growth enhancing environment in which to live!

A final note before we leave this chapter on relationships: All of us live in networks of relationships which begin with ourselves as individuals, touch family and friends closest to us, and include neighbors, membership groups, community, region, nation, hemisphere, world (even the universe?). In the 1980s we are witnessing a resurgence of nationalism throughout the world; it may be hoped that we do not lose sight of our *world citizenship* in the process. The earth is small; we can ill afford the arrogance and ethnocentricity of separation by political boundaries. Relationships with others begin at home, on the block, and down in town; but they must extend to our fellow human beings all over this tiny globe. At risk is our continued existence as a species.

14

Anger is Not a
Four-Letter Word

*When angry, count five; when very angry,
swear.*
— Mark Twain

The common confusion of angry *feelings* with aggressive *behavior* creates a tremendous barrier to expression of the natural, healthy, universal, and useful human emotion we call anger.

Some folks say, "I never get angry." We don't believe it! Everyone *gets* angry. Some people have so controlled themselves that they do not openly *show* anger. We are convinced that it's healthy to express anger, and that it can be done constructively. People who develop nondestructive assertive ways to deal with anger can make aggressive actions unnecessary in their lives.

All too often, people express anger, frustration, or disappointment with another person by indirect, hurtful methods. If the desired goal is to change the behavior of the intended target, these approaches are rarely successful.

Newlyweds Martha and John are a "classic" case. In the first few months of their marriage, Martha discovered at least a dozen of John's habits which she found objectionable. Unfortunately for both, she was unable — or unwilling — to

125

find the courage to confront John openly with her concerns. Martha instead chose the "safe" way to express her dissatisfaction with John's behavior; she confided in her mother. Worse yet, not content with almost daily telephone conversations with mother about John's shortcomings, she also used family get-togethers as occasions to berate John before the rest of the family.

This "see-how-bad-he-is" style — telling a third person (or persons) about your dislikes of another — may have disastrous effects upon a relationship. John feels hurt, embarrassed, and hostile about Martha's attacks. He wishes she had chosen the privacy of their own relationship to tell him of her annoyances. Instead of being motivated to change his habits, he responds to her aggressive approach with bitterness and a resolve to strike back by intensifying the very behaviors she would have him change.

Had Martha asserted herself directly by telling John of her feelings, she would have created a good foundation for a cooperative effort to modify both John's behavior and her inappropriate response to it.

If John had responded assertively early in the process he might have prevented the escalation of Martha's attacks, and avoided the bitterness and growing resentment. Instead, his determination to get revenge is sure to drive a further wedge into the relationship. John and Martha seem sure bets for the divorce court.

Adam took his car to a large repair shop for several hours of work. Maintenance in this shop is done on a first-come, first-served basis, and Adam arrived at 8 a.m. He told the manager he would pick the car up around 4:30 p.m.

When he came back, the following conversation took place:

Adam: "Hi. I'm Adam Z., and I'm here to pick up my car."

Manager (looking through his worksheets): "I'm sorry,

sir, we haven't gotten to your car yet.''

Adam: ''Damn! That really makes me mad! This is supposed to be first-come, first-served, and I was here at 8 a.m. What happened?''

Manager: ''Hey, it was one of those days. We put it in the back and got busy and just didn't get to it.''

Adam: ''Well, hell, that doesn't do me any good. It's an inconvenience for me to get my car in and leave it all day.''

Manager: ''I know that and I apologize. I promise to get it done first thing in the morning if you want to bring it back.''

At this point, Adam has a choice to make: get the manager to have someone fix his car by working overtime; take his car elsewhere; return the next day for the repair work; demand a loan car; become aggressive.

Adam so far has expressed his anger without being aggressive toward the manager. He was rightfully mad, and told the manager so without downgrading him as a person. He might have responded aggressively: ''You can take that repair job and shove it,'' and stormed out, or said, ''You damn S.O.B.s better fix my car *right now!*'' Either of these statements would likely inflame the manager and not accomplish much.

It is possible and desirable to express angry feelings without hurting someone (physically or emotionally) in the process. Honest and spontaneous expression can help to prevent inappropriate and destructive anger. It will often achieve your goals at the outset. Even when assertion doesn't gain what you're after, however, it still defuses the anger you might direct toward yourself if you had done nothing.

An important part of constructive anger expression to accept responsibility for your own feelings. *You* feel the anger, and that doesn't make the other person ''stupid,'' ''an S.O.B.,'' or the cause of your feeling.

Venting aggression (by hitting other people with foam bats or by shouting obscenities) is *not* psychologically healthy. Physical expression of hostility does nothing to solve the problem. Banging the table, stomping the floor, crying, striking at the air, hitting a pillow — all are devices for temporary release of strong feelings without aggression toward another person. However, they are not effective methods for dealing with your anger.

What's more, contrary to the popular myth, angry feelings are not "released" through aggressive acts — one simply learns to handle anger aggressively.

Let's take a closer look at what the most careful psychological research tells us about anger.

Facts, Theories, and Myths About Anger

We keep looking for the easy answers.

We elect officials who offer glib solutions to the incredibly complex issues of the day, as if the good guys and the bad guys could still be identified by the color of their hats. We try to oversimplify relationships between apparent "causes" and their "effects." We want the answer to "Why do I behave that way?" to be simply, "Because you were toilet trained too early." We search for effortless equations to "explain" the mysteries of human behavior.

Anger is one of those phenomena which is an easy target for such simplistic psychology. It is variously characterized as "sinful" (and therefore to be avoided at all costs), "freeing" (and therefore to be expressed at all costs), and all of the options in between.

Part of the reason for the lack of adequate explanations and methods for dealing with anger is that until very recently anger research has been limited and not very clear. A fairly consistent pattern of data is now emerging which could move us a giant step toward a theoretically sound and usable working model of anger.

On the following page is a table which summarizes some current notions about anger, classified under three headings: *facts* — findings which are clearly demonstrated by careful

ANGER: FACTS, THEORIES, AND MYTHS

FACTS	THEORIES	MYTHS
Anger is a feeling, with physiological components.	Shy people, depressed people, and suicides are expressing anger at themselves.	Venting (by yelling, pounding pillows, hitting with foam bats) "releases" anger and therefore "deals with" it.
Anger is not a mode of behavior.	Anger should always be expressed spontaneously/immediately.	Women are less angry than men.
Anger is universal among human beings.	Anger should always be contained until it can be expressed in a calm, rational manner.	Some people never get angry.
Nonexpression of anger leads to increased risk of coronary heart disease in both men and women.	Verbal expression of anger is always desirable.	Anger always results from frustration.
What really matters is resolving the issue. Thus, the method of anger expression is important.	Men in our culture are able to express anger more easily than women.	Anger is always a "secondary" emotion, with another "real" feeling behind it.
Venting of anger — "catharsis" — is of lasting value only insofar as it sets the stage for resolution.	Women are generally inhibited in anger expression by their social conditioning in our culture.	Aggressive behavior is a sure sign of an "angry person."
Aggressive expression leads to further aggressive expression, not resolution.		TV violence, active sports and/or competitive work "releases" anger.
Anger is not a "steam kettle" phenomenon; it does not build up and finally explode.		Aggressive behavior is instinctive in humans.
Most anger is directed toward those close to us, not strangers.		Anger is a destructive, sinful, undesirable emotion.

research, or are self-evident; *theories* — ideas for which there is some solid evidence, but which lack clear validation, and sometimes lead us astray; and *myths* — ideas which, despite their acceptance, have been proved wrong, or which appear on the surface to be accurate but contain false assumptions. The chart represents a summary of what is known about anger, according to the most recent careful studies. If you want to know more about anger, we suggest Dr. Carol Tavris' excellent book, *Anger: The Misunderstood Emotion.*

"I'm Afraid of My Buried Anger!"

Anger is a powerful influence on our capacity to understand and express feelings, and on our mental health in general. Yet, anger remains one of the most difficult emotions for many people to express. Our assertive behavior groups often lose members when assertive expression of anger becomes the topic. Many are simply afraid of their anger. Having "buried" it for years, they are terrified of the potential consequences should they suddenly "let it out."

In our experience, we've found the gradual freeing of anger expression can be frightening for some people. Not knowing any constructive, assertive approaches to express anger, they assume that any anger brought into the open will be hurtful to the other person. "I'd sooner suffer in silence than to hurt anyone," is the common, unfortunate plea.

Yet much pain in human relationships results from anger which is denied expression. Both persons suffer. The angry one silently fumes. The other person continues to behave in ways which are upsetting, and wonders why the relationship is deteriorating.

You Are Not A Steam Kettle!

An important distinction must be made here. Recent research has shown the popular concept of our emotions as a "steam kettle" to be false. Many people have believed that by *expressing* anger, the anger would go away and prevent the problems associated with "building up inside." We now know that anger expression is only the beginning.

What happens is that we *remember* annoying events, and our feelings of anger can be experienced again when those memories are tapped. But there are important differences between a "steam kettle" of simmering emotion and a "memory bank" of stored experiences. Effective dealing with stored anger does not mean pounding a pillow until you are exhausted; it means working out some *resolution* of the issue yourself — through negotiation, confrontation, forgiveness, attitude change, or psychotherapy.

Emotional relief from anger comes only when expression is accompanied by some resolution of the problem which caused the anger. Getting the feelings out — even in appropriately assertive ways — only "sets the stage." Working out the conflict with the other person, or within yourself, is the all-important step which makes the difference.

Lack of such coping or resolution action may actually increase anger *whether it has been expressed or not.* So, get your anger out, but follow up your (assertive) release of feelings with problem-solving actions which will help to resolve the issue. You may work toward assertive negotiation of solutions with the person with whom you have been angry, or you may sometimes find satisfaction within yourself (perhaps with the aid of a therapist or trusted friend). In either event, don't stop by saying, "I'm mad as hell!" Follow through with "...and here's what I think we can do about it..."

"Why Do I Get So Angry?"

Here are some elements to look for as you answer that question for yourself:

Your Environment. First, let's set the scene. Where do you get angry? Consider the temperature, pollution, weather. Were you caught in a traffic jam? Pushed around in a crowd? Waiting in a slow line? Do you live under political oppression?

(It's not hard to understand the anger of Blacks in South Africa!) Economic hardship? (An economic depression can make it tough to feel good.) Are you a member of a minority which is often treated unfairly? (Women, Blacks, Native Americans, Hispanics, Jews, gays... lots of folks have good reasons to *start the day* angry.)

Yourself. How's your health? Any significant disabilities? Are you fatigued much of the time? Under tension? Do you eat a balanced nutritious diet? Have you had a physical exam recently enough to be sure that your internal chemistry is right? Any of those factors can make it more likely that you will get angry if the right situation comes along.

Your attitudes and expectations. Do you believe the world should treat you fairly? Is it important to you to have people recognize your accomplishments? Do you have a strong sense of justice? Are there certain "right" ways things should be done? Rules everybody should live by? Such attitudes, beliefs, and expectations — while very human — can set you up to get angry at the way the real world treats you and others.

Your job. Do you work with unreasonable people? Are you happy in your personal and intimate relationships? Is your work satisfying and rewarding? If you are *out* of a job, you may be close to anger all the time.

"*So What Can I Do About My Anger?*"

There *are* constructive ways to handle anger. Here's our view of a healthy approach to dealing with anger:

Before you get angry

(1) Recognize, and allow yourself to believe, that anger is a natural, healthy, non-evil human feeling. Everyone feels it, we just don't all *express* it. You needn't fear your anger.

(2) Remember that *you* are responsible for your own feelings. You got angry at what happened; the other person didn't "make" you angry.

(3) Remember that anger and aggression are not the same thing! Anger can be expressed assertively.

(4) Get to know yourself. Recognize the attitudes, environments, events, and behaviors which trigger your anger. As some say, "Find your own buttons, so you'll know when they're pushed!" (Take another look at the preceding section.)

(5) Don't "set yourself up" to get angry! If your temperature rises when you must wait in a slow line (at the bank, in traffic), work at finding alternate ways to accomplish those tasks (bank by mail, find another route to work, use the time for problem solving).

(6) Learn to relax. Develop the skill of relaxing yourself, and learn to apply it when your anger is triggered. You may wish to take this a step further by "desensitizing" yourself to certain anger-invoking situations (see Chapter 10).

(7) Develop several coping strategies for handling your anger, including relaxation, physical exertion, "stress inoculation" statements, working out resolution within yourself, and other procedures noted in the list at the end of this chapter. Focus on relationship goals and assertive methods.

(8) Develop and practice assertive methods for *expressing* your anger, following the principles described in this book: be spontaneous; don't wait and build resentment; state your anger directly; avoid sarcasm and innuendo; use honest, expressive language; avoid namecalling, putdowns, physical attacks, one-upmanship, hostility. Some of the verbal expressions others have found useful include:

"I'm very angry."
"I'm getting really mad."
"I strongly disagree with you."
"I get damn mad when you say that."
"I'm very disturbed by this whole thing."
"Stop bothering me."
"That's not fair."

"Don't do that."
"That really pisses me off."
"You have no right to do that."
"I really don't like that."
"I'm mad as hell, and I'm not going to take this anymore!"

(9) Develop and practice assertive methods for *resolution* of your anger. Take responsibility for your own feelings and attitudes. Apply conflict management strategies (later in this chapter). Listen nondefensively. Be aware of your own attitudes which may have set up your angry reaction. Be specific. Seek solutions, not blame.

Take some time to examine the role anger is playing in your life. Make some notes in your log about what sets you up to get angry, and what you'd like to do about it. Then go on to the following section and read our ideas for handling your anger when it comes.

When you get angry:
(10) Apply the coping strategies you developed in step **7** above, and those listed at the end of the chapter.

(11) Take a few moments to consider if this situation is really worth your time and energy, and the possible consequences of expressing yourself.

If you decide to take action:
(12) Make some verbal expression of concern (assertively).

(13) Take a few more moments to decide if this situation is one you wish to work out with the other person, or one you will resolve within yourself.

(14) "Schedule" time for working things out. If you are able to do so spontaneously, fine; if not, arrange a time (with the other person or with yourself) to deal with the issue later. (See also (19) below.).

(15) State your feelings directly, with appropriate nonverbal cues (if you are genuinely angry, a smile is inappropriate!).

(16) Accept responsibility for your feelings. (See (2) above).

(17) Stick to specifics and to the present situation. Avoid generalizing about the entire history of your relationship!

All the time:

(18) Work toward *resolution,* not "victory."

(19) Keep your life clear! Deal with issues when they arise, when you feel the feelings — not after hours/days/weeks of "stewing" about it. When you can't deal with it immediately, arrange a specific time when you can and will!

Go ahead! Get angry! But develop a positive, assertive style for expressing it. You, and those around you, will appreciate it.

When Somebody Else Is Angry With You

Okay, now you know how to deal with your own anger. But one of the most important needs expressed by assertiveness trainees is for ways to deal with the anger of *others*. What can you do when someone is furious and directing their full hostility at you?

Try these steps:

• Allow the angry person to vent the strong feelings.

• Respond only with acceptance at first ("It's obvious that you're really upset about this.")

• Take a deep breath, and try to stay as calm as possible.

• Offer to discuss a solution later — giving the person time to cool off ("I think we both need some time to think about this. I'd like to talk with you about it ...in an hour/ ...tomorrow/...next week.")

• Take another deep breath.

- Arrange a specific time to pursue the matter.
- Keep in mind that no immediate solution is likely.
- Follow the conflict resolution strategies described below, when you meet to follow up.

Constructive Resolution of Anger and Conflict

How can we improve the process of resolving angry conflict between people or groups? Most of the principles are parallel to the methods of assertiveness training presented throughout this book, and many overlap our discussion earlier in this chapter of ways to deal with anger.

Conflict is more easily resolved when both parties...

...act honestly and directly toward one another.

...are willing to face the problem openly, rather than avoiding or hiding from it.

...avoid personal attacks; stick to the issues.

...emphasize points of agreement as a foundation for discussion of points of argument.

...employ a "rephrasing" style of communication, to be sure you understand each other. ("Let me see if I understand you correctly. Do you mean...?")

...accept responsibility for their own feelings ("I am angry!" not "You made me mad!").

...avoid a "win-lose" position. The attitude that "I am going to win, and you are going to lose" will more likely result in *both* losing. By remaining flexible, both can win — at least in part.

...gain the same information about the situation. Because perceptions so often differ, it is good to make everything explicit.

...develop goals which are basically compatible. If we both want to preserve the relationship more than to win, we have a better chance!

...clarify their actual needs in the situation. I probably don't need to *win*. I do need to gain some specific outcome (behavior change by you, more money), and to retain my self-respect.

...seek solutions rather than deciding who is to blame.

...agree upon some means of negotiation or exchange. I probably would agree to give on some points if you would give on some!

...negotiate toward a mutually acceptable compromise, or simply agree to disagree.

When conflict involves strong angry feelings, many people fear bringing those feelings into the open, perhaps because they have been told since early childhood that anger is bad. Recognizing the value of anger, allowing that natural feeling to be expressed nondestructively, and working toward resolution of the problem will create the conditions necessary for constructive conflict resolution, and healthy, growing relationships.

EFFECTIVE TECHNIQUES FOR COPING
WITH ANGER

- Keep an anger diary.
- Write a self-management contract, including vows and affirmations to yourself.
- Learn alternative behaviors to undertake when feeling angry.
- Learn to ignore or "tune out" provocation.
- Develop early warning systems:
    - Know your own "buttons"
    - Know your body feelings
- Count to ten, to delay your response.
- Develop a relaxation response to employ when you begin to feel angry or annoyed.
- Focus on the task at hand and your goals.
- Leave the anger-invoking situation.
- Talk yourself out of feeling angry.
- Exaggerate your feelings to a ridiculous extreme — then laugh at yourself.
- Look for humor in the situation.
- Develop cool, friendly ways of responding to potential angry situations, or hostility in others.
- Read a lot about dealing with anger — especially in history and great literature and ancient philosophy.
- Learn stress inoculation techniques.
- Develop a rational belief system — overcome irrational beliefs such as "the world should be fair."
- Learn how to express anger assertively.

15

Must We Put Up
With Put Downs?

*He that respects himself is safe from others;
he wears a coat of mail that none can pierce.*
— Henry Wadsworth Longfellow

Remember those times in life when you felt belittled by somebody? The feeling may have resulted from a look, expression or shrug. Or someone's words may have provoked a feeling of worthlessness.

You feel perplexed! Instead of feeling up, you start to doubt yourself and feel down. Put-downs provoke a cloud of darkness or confusion and may stand out in your mind for years.

You say, "Of course there are a lot of put-downs. That's because there is so much to criticize!" Perhaps. People do scowl at looks, dress, lifestyle, mannerisms, work performance, speech. It is easy to come up with ways to let others know they are not O.K.

Most of us add to the problem of put-downs from others by automatically putting down ourselves as well. If you were out in the woods all alone eating lunch and accidentally dropped your sandwich, what would you do? Some caustic comment about your good sense likely would be heard echoing through the trees, or at least through the channels of your mind. We tend to compound what others think of us by self put-downs.

Let's explore these different put-down behaviors and what to do about them: the direct verbal put-down; the indirect verbal putdown; the nonverbal putdown; and the self put-down.

The Direct Verbal Put-Down

This type of behavior is obvious: another person is verbally "blasting" you. Imagine, for example, that you have just come out of an elevator and accidentally brushed against someone. That person responds immediately in a hostile manner: "Damn it! Why don't you watch it! You fool! You could have hurt me!" The intent is quite upfront, isn't it? How should you respond to such an overreaction to an innocent gesture on your part? There is certainly no need to guess about the meaning of the reaction!

Here are the steps we have found effective in dealing with a direct verbal put-down:

- allow the person to slow down or vent feelings;
- admit when you are wrong, even in the face of insult;
- acknowledge the other person's feelings;
- assert yourself about the way he or she is reacting;
- make a short statement to bring the encounter to an end.

These steps will help resolve a put-down encounter where the intent is out in the open.

In the elevator incident you could first let the person vent until the angry feelings slow down. As the outburst subsides, you could say, "I apologize for brushing against you. It was accidental. Obviously you are upset, but I don't like to be called names or yelled at. I can get your point without that." This is just one example of a way to apply the steps suggested above.

Indirect Verbal Put-Downs

How about this one, from your boss? "You did a nice job on that project you turned in yesterday. All the grammatical errors gave it a folksy quality." Or, what if your spouse says, "I love the way you look when you wear that outfit; old clothes become you." Do you do a double-take? Are you confused? What are the real meanings behind statements of this kind?

Such indirect verbal put-downs are *indirect aggression.* In their book, *The Assertive Woman*, Stanlee Phelps and Nancy Austin describe indirect aggressive behavior by observing: "...in order to achieve her goal, she may use trickery, seduction, or manipulation." They note that others react with confusion, frustration, and a feeling of being manipulated. Indirect aggressive behavior comes out as a concealed attack; Phelps and Austin label the person who behaves in this manner a "mad dog in a lamb's suit."

Handle an indirect verbal put-down first by asking for more information. In either of the situations given above, you might reply with, "What are you saying?" or "What do you mean?" Such a response tends to help clarify the person's true intent (You may have misunderstood!)

Your second response will depend upon the other person's answer. Part of your goal in the situation, however, is to teach the person a new way of behaving toward you. If the boss indicates on the second exchange that, "Oh, I think you did a good job," you might still want to say, "Well, thank you, but I was a little confused. If you're really concerned about my errors in grammar, I hope you'll say so directly. I couldn't really tell if you thought the project was good or bad." You are trying to teach the boss to be straightforward with you.

In marriage relationships, some good-natured teasing can be fun. Too often, however, underlying hostilities come out in the guise of teasing. Your spouse may have been kidding you all along, but there are more straightforward and less destructive ways to do so.

What if your spouse is not kidding? And imagine that the next response from your boss is even more aggressive. Any indirect verbal put-down could lead to a direct verbal put-down. After you ask the person to clarify, the next response may be even worse. We suggest that you remain assertive, following the steps given above for direct verbal put-downs. Be prepared to go further with your assertion if the response to your inquiry is another put-down.

On the other hand, when you ask for clarification, you may hear some valuable information from the other person about your behavior. Remember that a major goal of assertive behavior is that *both* people can express themselves openly and honestly. It is difficult for most of us to give direct feedback about another person's upsetting behavior. This is usually the reason we camouflage comments by an indirect put-down style. Digging further may help your future relationship with that person.

Nonverbal Put-Downs

"Sticks and stones may break my bones, but words will never hurt me" is a taunt children long have used to rebuff name-callers. Unfortunately, no reply has yet been invented for our adversaries who put us down *without* words. What is the best way to respond to an obscene gesture or a dirty look? How should pouting and silly grins or smirks be dealt with when the person uses no words to help you verify the intention precisely?

The nonverbal put-down is much harder to deal with because there are no words in the first place, and the person may not even be consciously aware of the put-down. Moreover, you cannot be certain you accurately read the nonverbal message.

If another person aims an obviously *aggressive* nonverbal put-down toward you, try to get the person to use words instead of gestures. You might say assertively, "Could you translate that look (gesture) into words for me? I have trouble knowing what you're feeling unless you tell me directly.'' Be prepared for a verbal put-down at this point and respond according to the suggestions given above.

The *nonassertive* nonverbal put-down is the least direct of all. You aren't likely to misinterpret the meaning when someone aggressively shakes a fist in your face! However, if you are making a request of someone who begins to stare off into space or grins inappropriately, the intent is not so obvious. There is a good chance that the person who responds with an indirect nonverbal put-down is doing so automatically, out of habit. We all have mannerisms which take the place of words. Although it is not possible to eliminate all nonverbal messages, we feel that it is best to put them into words if there is a chance they might be misinterpreted.

Imagine that you are about to pay for a purchase when the cashier looks at you, grimaces, and sighs in an exasperated way. You may wish to write this off as nothing personal, or merely assume the cashier is having a bad day. If you are bothered by the incident, however, why not deal with it directly? Ask the person to explain: "I didn't understand your expression," or, "I'm not sure what you mean by that," or, "Did I do something you didn't like?" This places the nonverbal response out in the open, to clear the air.

If you have done something that bothers somebody else, you deserve to know. Your next response will depend on what happens then, but we think it is a good idea to point out that it's difficult to interpret such nonverbal messages.

The Self Put-Down

Outer conflict, such as that described above, is only half of the picture. Inner conflict can also result in put-downs. The offender in this case is yourself. Put-downs are generated by conflicts, external or internal. The solution is the same — be assertive.

You can behave non-assertively or aggressively within

yourself as well as toward others. Be careful about how you deal with yourself. Try not to (nonassertively) take flight and neglect or escape your inner put-down behavior. Don't be too (aggressively) caustic and condemning with your inner thoughts and feelings either. Take the middle ground: deal with yourself assertively. Be honest, open, straightforward with yourself. Don't condemn or run away from put-downs, your own or another's.

Summary

No one likes the conflict generated by put-downs. By risking an open and straightforward clarification, with the other person or yourself, the discord can usually be resolved.

It does take some constraint to avoid feeling hurt and withdrawing or lashing out. The rewards of honest communication are often well worth the effort.

The upset caused by put-downs can be resolved if you will put your "assertive foot forward." Be persistent in clarifying the situation with yourself or the other person, and reap the benefits of clearing the air, expressing your feelings, gaining new information about yourself and your relationships, and resolving the real or imagined conflict.

16

Assertiveness Works
at Work, Too

*Worthy are the labors which give us a sign other
than age to show that we have lived.*
— Leon Batista Alberti

To be assertive on the job can be particularly difficult. Fear of
reprisals from supervisors or co-workers, even fear of losing
the job itself, are formidable obstacles for many.

Yet there are countless ways to express yourself
assertively at work. In this chapter, we'll explore several,
including some examples to help you see how assertiveness
can work for you.

We've arranged this material in its natural sequence,
from the process of job and career search, through landing a
job, working well with others, to being a supervisor. The
chapter concludes with some questions about your priorities,
and a potpourri of work situations for your own assertiveness
practice. It may help to read all of the material, or you may
prefer to turn directly to that aspect of job-related
assertiveness which fits your specific interests and needs.

Job Search

When we graduated from college in the late 1950s, jobs were plentiful for anyone with a degree. Things have changed a lot in the last quarter century; jobs can be tough to get in many fields these days, with or without a college education.

Looking for a job can be a full time "job" in itself. Too many people seem to expect to put out a few applications, make a few calls, have an interview or two, and land the job of their dreams. Unfortunately, that *is* a dream. Finding work takes work — and assertiveness can be one of your most useful tools.

Richard Nelson Bolles, in his bestselling book *What Color Is Your Parachute?*, presents a comprehensive plan for "Job Seekers and Career Changers." His counsel is as good as you'll find anywhere, and applies the concepts of assertiveness with a broad brush. Bolles' innovative and practical ideas will help you learn about your own career desires and needs, locate opportunities, make contact with employers, handle interviews, and land the job you want.

Among Bolles' recommendations for an assertive approach to careers:

• Plan your career and your job search with a clear goal in mind: decide what you want to do, where you want to do it, and for whom.

• Seek out activities you enjoy: you'll go after them with more enthusiasm, do them better, and be satisfied longer.

• Claim the highest level of skill you legitimately can: you are more likely to find a job and the job can be more uniquely tailored to you.

• Find and meet the employer you want to work for: show the person who has the power to hire you just how you can help fill the needs of that organization.

Interviewing

Even if you have followed Bolles' advice and created your

own job, you'll likely go through some traditional interviews along the way.

Now at last an employer has offered you an opportunity to meet and discuss an opening! You've worked hard for this chance to tell what you can do, and you are really looking forward to it. You are pretty anxious, too. After all, getting the job depends largely upon how well you present yourself in that short meeting.

Assertiveness can help. We suggest you take it as it comes:

Before the interview...

...Follow the principles we've described in this book to develop your own assertive skills.

...Prepare yourself to deal with anxiety by practicing relaxation and cognitive restructuring (Chapters 9 and 10).

...Write down and memorize three or four key strengths you want to be sure the interviewer remembers about you; be sure to relate them specifically to the job in question.

...Practice interviewing with a friend or counselor. If you can, use a video recorder and camera to capture a sample of your own style. Watch the tape, and use that feedback to help you become even more effective.

At the interview...

...Approach the interviewer with a friendly, not-*too*-well-rehearsed style.

...Remember that most employers would rather hire someone with a strong desire to work and to contribute to the organization than a "star" who may try to outshine the current staff.

...Try to relax, enjoy yourself, and get acquainted!

...Let the interviewer know that you've done your homework, prepared for the interview, and learned something about the company.

...Ask good questions about the working environment, staff morale, advancement, employer expectations.

...Avoid asking obvious questions you should have answered

for yourself by some advance preparation (company product line, details about retirement and health benefits...).

...Leave the interviewer with a sample of your work, or some other device which will cause him or her to remember you and your talents.

After the interview...

...Drop a note to the interviewer, expressing your appreciation for the meeting, calling attention to any important facts about you, and mentioning details which may have been missed in the interview.

...Spend some time assessing and critiquing your own performance, so you'll be ready to do even better next time.

...Continue to contact other employers and to arrange other interviews until you land the job *you* want!

Can The "New Kid On The Block" Be Assertive?

When you do get that new job, it is important to start out by *listening* a lot. You'll need to find out as much as possible about the rules of the workplace, the attitudes and opinions of your supervisors and colleagues, the safety factors of the job, the expectations of your role and how it fits into the larger scheme of things, and much more.

But listening probably will not be enough to give you all the information you'll need. As you begin to learn your way around a new place of employment, it will be important to ask questions as well. And that's where assertiveness comes in once again.

Remember to maintain *balance*. You want to seem interested in the job, to show the boss and others that you are conscientious. At the same time, you don't want to be a constant nag, demanding more and more information — much of which may not even be relevant to your own work.

We suggest the following guidelines:

...Ask your supervisor and co-workers the questions to which you *must* have answers in order to do the job.

...Don't be *too* quick to ask, since you may be told when the subject comes up in turn.

...Make notes of other items which occur to you, and ask them when the subject comes up.

...Ask your boss about *asking* questions: Does she/he prefer that you ask immediately, or in a regular conference, or when...?

...Do your homework. Don't expect your boss or co-workers to fill the gaps in your own *preparation* for the job (unless you are clearly in a training program).

...When you do ask questions, be assertive: don't beat around the bush, don't start out defensively ("This may be a dumb question..."), try to focus your question on the specifics, use good eye contact, voice, timing, etc.

...Avoid suggesting changes until you are well acquainted with the operation.

...Avoid the temptation to describe "how we did it at Acme Widget" (or wherever you've worked before) unless you're asked. Better to let it be your own idea — or let it go altogether.

On-The-Job Relationships

Getting along with others at work is essentially a process of making a place for yourself in the work group. At home, the family has little choice but to accept you. In school, although acceptance of your peers can be a tough burden, *you*'re the one without choice: you *have* to be there.

The job, for most of us, does offer some choices. Unlike family or school ties, one *can* quit, although the price for doing so may be high. Getting along becomes a matter of deciding to make that place for yourself. And that means developing a relationship of mutual respect with your co-workers.

Here are some ideas which may help:

...stay honest; avoid game playing.

...count to ten before you sound off in anger (refer to Chapter 14).

...listen to what the other person has to say — even if you disagree.

...ask yourself "How would *I* feel in that person's shoes?"

...express your opinions, but remember they are opinions, not gospel.

...consider: is it more important to be a "star," or to get the job done?

...be assertive when it matters.

...accept responsibility for your mistakes — and credit for your successes.

A couple of practice situations for you to think about:

...A co-worker has been taking company supplies home for personal use. She knows you are aware of this, and expects you to say nothing.

...The woman at the next desk loves to chew gum — loudly. You find the noise annoying and distracting.

Dealing With Supervisors

Some bosses act as though they would have been happier in an earlier era, when all employees were virtual slaves. For the most part, however, the workplace has become quite civilized — even humanized. Supervisors still oversee, but they generally follow modern law and custom — and their own good sense — in treating their workers with respect.

Nevertheless, there are inevitable situations in which it is necessary, as an employee, to express an idea, opinion, or objection firmly, in the face of opposition from the boss.

Don't get caught in the trap of coming down on yourself every time you are criticized on the job. You may be wrong, but the way to deal with the situation is to correct the problem, not to kick yourself. Help your boss to make criticism *specific*, so you can make the adjustments needed to improve.

Assertive efforts to clarify the boss's expectations and criticisms will help clear the air, and will enable you to become more effective. If instead you act as a "victim" —

mumbling to yourself or backbiting — you'll make no progress, and likely make a powerful enemy along the way.

Try to identify *patterns* in your boss's critiques. If you think you discover one, ask assertively if that *is* what the boss wants ("You'd rather have all the supporting data presented *with* my recommendations, wouldn't you?"). If you clear up any possible misunderstanding in this direct way, you'll save time — and similar criticism — in the future.

Timing may be the most important component of your on-the-job assertiveness — especially with the boss. If you confront a supervisor in front of others, or when the boss is very preoccupied with another problem, you aren't likely to gain a favorable audience. Instead, plan — and schedule if necessary — your feedback to the boss so that you can be alone and relatively uninterrupted.

Here are a few other examples of situations with supervisors for practice:

...You have an innovative suggestion for simplifying a routine procedure.

...Your boss is making unreasonable demands on your time, without offering additional compensation.

...You are being unfairly criticized for the quality of your work.

...You know more about the job than your boss does, yet she wants you to do it her way.

...Your boss is asking you to do jobs which you believe are his responsibility.

...Your boss expects you to prepare "phony" expense accounts.

...You've been asked — at 4:45 — to stay this evening and prepare a report for tomorrow's Board meeting. You have plans for the evening.

Supervising Assertively

Now you've done it! You've been so effective with your on-the-job assertion (along with some pretty good work!) that you've been promoted. Now *you're* the boss. New responsibilities, new opportunities, ...new headaches!

How do the principles of assertiveness apply in the supervisory role? Can you get the job done, treat your staff with respect, and exercise appropriate authority — all at once?

There are many theories of management, and hundreds of good ideas about how to supervise others. While this is not the place for a comprehensive survey, the following guidelines blend our concept of assertiveness with some of the best:

...Build your assertive managerial style on the foundation of good on-the-job relationships described earlier in this chapter: honesty, responsibility, cooperation, teamwork, mutual respect.

...Listen — and pay attention — to what your people have to say.

...Roll up your own sleeves and work *with* your staff.

...Walk around — find out first hand what is needed.

...Remember: we're all equal on the human-to-human level.

...Make your instructions clear and direct.

...Accept the responsibility of leadership, including decision-making.

...Criticize fairly, focussing on the performance — not the person.

...Praise often, focussing on the performance — not the person.

...Consider: a manager must both *lead* the staff and provide necessary *support*.

Here are a few supervisory situations for practice — and to help you keep things in perspective:

...One of your employees has made a thoughtful proposal for a new work procedure. You recognize the idea as one the General Manager would probably veto because of its start-up costs.

...A supervisor of your rank from another department comes

into your area and wants to borrow some tools. Company policy prohibits such transfers.

...As a first-line supervisor, you are confronted by a young trainee who refuses to obey your directions.

...An employee under your supervision is not working up to your standards. You wish to improve his performance.

...Performance reviews are due next week. You must critique two people whose work is weak in several areas.

...As a new lead-man at an assembly plant, you are responsible for the work of several men old enough to be your father. At least one of the men believes his ways are right, and refuses to accept your authority.

...A long-time employee in your department has been coming to work late nearly every day this week, with no explanation.

...You recognize that one of your workers is an alcoholic, but she won't admit it or seek treatment.

Keeping Your Priorities Straight

Work can be really seductive. If you enjoy what you do, and if you are good at it, you'll probably be advancing in salary and responsibility frequently. As a result, you'll feel motivated to take on even more, and the cycle will go on.

That sort of involvement with your work can play havoc with your personal life — if you let it get out of hand. More and more, you'll take work home, stay late at the job, go in weekends, take business trips. You could wind up with little time left for yourself or your family.

Can you be assertive with yourself? Can you elect to pass up career advancement opportunities in favor of more time for home and family? What are your priorities? It's easy to *say*, "My family comes first." It's harder to act accordingly.

Others won't settle for less than "having it all." Career, family, community, self — all are juggled like oranges, at least for a while. The stresses of the real world seldom allow us to maintain that precarious balance for long.

Being assertive with yourself means clarifying your personal priorities, recognizing you cannot do everything — at least not all the time — making appropriate choices, and saying "no" when you've reached your limits. Keep your own goals in mind (refer to Chapter 8 and your log as you need to).

Test yourself with a few related situations. What's *really* important to you?

...You've been offered an important promotion with your present firm. Actually, you had been thinking of leaving, but the outside job you want is not yet available.

...More and more evenings and weekends are spent working on job reports. Your family is beginning to complain that you have no time for them. You think you have an opportunity for a major promotion if you keep up the pace.

...You want to continue your successful career, but you know that your only step up in the company will require going back to school for additional course work in business — maybe an MBA. Such a step will require postponing plans to have children — which you and your husband want very much.

More On The Job Situations For Practice

Use the step-by-step process in Chapter 12 as a guide to build your skills, and practice handling the following work-related situations:

...Your boss suddenly turns cool toward you, but offers no explanation. You want to ask what's going on.

...Although you have been in your job longer than anyone in your department, you are a part-time worker. Nevertheless, you are often called upon to train others or answer questions as if you were a supervisor. You are paid less, and have no real authority.

...You've had several job interviews recently, but keep finding yourself acting in a very passive way. The interviewers seem disappointed that you do not "sell" yourself.

...A manager in another department — very powerful in the

company — has been making not-so-subtle sexual advances to you.

...After you've spent many hours on a special project, your boss's supervisor is highly critical of your results.

...You've been asked to handle a job which is clearly outside your responsibility and beyond your competence. You think it may be a "test" of how well you know your own limits.

Even if you are not working regularly now, chances are you will be sooner or later. Give some thought to the issues raised in this chapter. Use your log to keep track of your own on-the-job assertiveness, and how you can improve it. You'll be more effective in your work, more highly respected by your peers and supervisors, and enjoy yourself more!

17

Assertion and Sexuality

> *Live all you can; it's a mistake not to. It doesn't so much matter what you do in particular, so long as you have had your life. If you haven't had that, what have you had?*
>
> — William James

Assertiveness and sexuality may seem to be strange bedfellows (pun fully intended!), but the two subjects actually have a lot to do with each other.

Human sexuality weaves together the individual, the couple, and the society in a highly complex fabric of attitudes, emotions, physiology, mores, customs, values — even politics and economics. And your own personal sexuality is uniquely intricate. "Everyone knows that," you say, "Nobody ever said it would be easy." True, but most of us tend to forget it, and that's when many of our sexual troubles start.

In 1975, the World Health Organization recognized the complexity in a formal definition of sexual well-being:

Sexual health is the integration of the somatic, emotional, intellectual, and social aspects of sexual being, in ways that are positively enriching and that enhance personality, communication, and love.

No other person has a body just like yours, of course, and that somatic uniqueness has a direct and diverse influence on your sexuality.

The emotional, intellectual, and social aspects of sexuality each make their contributions as well. What are the important beliefs, attitudes, behaviors that come through in *your* sexual expression? How do your friendships, family relationships, job, ideas about life, and feelings about yourself affect your sexual expression — or lack of it? And what about cultural influences? Your religion, ethnicity, even your politics may have something to say about how you express yourself sexually.

Communication is the essence of sexuality, and intimate communication is itself pretty complicated. Both partners are trying to make the best possible impression; things are not necessarily as they seem. Real feelings are hidden; sometimes we deceive even ourselves. We humans seem to be experts at being who we are not in our sexual communication and expression.

Arnold Lazarus, psychologist and faculty member at Rutgers, has recently identified two-dozen ''myths'' which create major problems in many relationships. In his book, *Marital Myths,* Lazarus suggests that the myth, ''True lovers automatically know each other's thoughts and feelings,'' is particularly destructive of sexual relationships. Don't take it for granted! Don't assume! Communicate!

What a confusing mess! You'd think that the complexity of sexual expression combined with the complexity of intimate communication would be enough to deter any sane person from engaging in either, let alone both!

But it doesn't, of course.

Is the Revolution Over?

In the past two decades there has been much emphasis on techniques of better sex. Kinsey may have started us off, but it was Masters and Johnson who guided us through the physical revolution stage.

Now the media has proclaimed the "sexual revolution" over. *Time* magazine devoted a 1984 cover story to the reduction of America's obsession with pure sex. We have moved from a time of heavy emphasis on the physical aspects of sex to a focus on the relationship aspects. Instead of exploring for new erogenous zones, we are talking about true intimacy, about devotion and commitment.

Some see this as a swing back to the "good old days." It seems more accurate to consider the entire process an evolution, of which the "revolution" was a key part. The new emphasis on commitment incorporates the gains made through increased sexual expression. There is no return to the old times, or forgetting about recent discoveries.

The revolution dug deeply at the closely-held attitudes, beliefs, stereotypes, and behaviors which inhibited complete sexual expression. Although traditional values were questioned, they were not abandoned. Now we are moving ahead with newfound abilities, openness, awareness, and equality.

The *Female and Male Sexual Attitudes and Behaviors* chart on the following page summarizes society's former and current sexual expectations for men and women. And the process of change continues.

FEMALE AND MALE SEXUAL ATTITUDES

AND BEHAVIORS

Females

Former Expectation	*Current Expectation*
Passivity	Equality
Misguided Compassion	No-nonsense Compassion
Silence and Suffering	Outspoken Enjoyment
Giving In	Initiation
Doing Your Duty	Active Participation
Hinting	Straightforwardness
Manipulation	Honesty
Shyness, Embarrassment	Confidence, Playfulness
Fragility, Weakness	Strength, Helpfulness

Males

Former Expectation	*Current Expectation*
Silence	Expression
Lack of Emotion	Openness, Flow
Insulation	Involvement
Strength	Vulnerability
Control	Mutuality
Machismo	Gentleness
Inflexibility	Patience
Exploitation	Equality
Score Keeping	Responsiveness

Both sexes are still overcoming blocks to healthy sexuality. Couples today are able to build their sexual relationships on the foundation of new knowledge and techniques, greater freedom of sexual expression, and a new equality between the sexes.

Where are we headed? The cornerstones of the new sexuality are communication and commitment. The new vocabulary includes words like assertiveness, adult-to-adult, negotiation, devotion, faithfulness, fidelity, and intimacy. We are entering a new era of togetherness... and taking with us the new knowledge about the physical aspects of sex.

Assertive Sexuality

In earlier chapters, we discussed self-expression as a need of all humans. Sexual expression is a special application of the principles of assertiveness we have presented throughout *Your Perfect Right*. Anxiety, skills, attitudes, obstacles... all are elements of sexual communication, along with the components of verbal and non-verbal behavior described in Chapter 6. What you have already learned about assertiveness is a good foundation for your assertive sexual communication.

One element which does seem to come up more frequently in sexual relationships than elsewhere is indirect aggression — so-called "passive-aggressive behavior." This is the style which is designed to make the other person feel guilty or bad, or to put responsibility on the other, or to manipulate the other into doing something. A variety of inventive methods are employed: false flattery, coyness, pouting, seeking sympathy, whining, crying, finding fault, playing "hard to get," even lying.

The *Sexual Communication Types* chart depicts four styles for expressing feelings about sexual interaction. For each style, five subcategories help narrow down our meaning: trait descriptions, inner thoughts, outer expressions, affect, body language.

SEXUAL COMMUNICATION TYPES

Behavior	Trait Descriptions	Inner Thoughts
Nonassertive	Hesitant, Shy	"She's being way too rough with me during sex."
		"He hurt my feelings when he said I wasn't much into sex tonight."
Indirectly Aggressive	Devious, Manipulative, Sneaky	(Upset that he's been told no) "I'll get her goat... insinuate she's been having an affair."
		"Ugh, sex tonight! I'll pretend to be terribly ill."
Aggressive	Demanding, Pushy, Insistent	"That's a stupid way to caress me!"
		"Why doesn't he ever want to have intercourse a different way? He is so straight!"
Assertive	Honest, Open, Straight-forward	"Our foreplay has been really short recently."
		"She hasn't seemed to be as responsive to me lately."

Outer Expressions	Affect	Body Language
"Did you think you were a little bit rough tonight?"	Irritated	Obscure
"I'm sorry, I wasn't very good tonight."		Hidden
"Did you read in the paper that people who aren't interested in much sex with their spouses are usually having affairs?"	Angry	Incongruent
Yawns, looks distressed, sighs, frequently rubs the stomach area.		Subversive
"You're so clumsy tonight!"	Hostile	Abrasive
"Are you crazy? Everyone is into this!"		Confrontive
"It seems to me that foreplay hasn't been very long lately. I enjoy it and would like it to last longer."	Bright	Forthright
"I have been feeling that you aren't as responsive during intercourse lately."		Direct

There are several important considerations to keep in mind about the four types of sexual communication:

First, none of us is purely one type or another. Each person may lean heavily one way, but we all exhibit all four behaviors at times. Come on now, admit it, even you! You have been known to pout a little or come on too strong or ineptly fumble around, haven't you? And, of course, there are times when you are quite confident, direct and assured. We would all like to be purely assertive, but no one is perfect!

Second, the goal in sexual communication is to have the capability and choice to respond as you like. Many of us respond by default, lacking the skills, attitudes, or behaviors necessary to be fully aware and in control of our sexual expressions. Those who keep working at it, however, do begin to find their relationships more satisfying and fulfilling.

Third, the motivation for some behavior is beyond our awareness. We fool ourselves. Of course, we think that we always understand why we react in certain ways, but depth psychology indicates differently. Feelings that are unresolved seem to appear in unexpected forms of behavior.

Fourth, all sexual communication is two-way, of mutual concern. This brings us back to devotion and commitment. Keep in mind your purpose. It isn't manipulation, or deceit, or always pleasing the other person, or being right. It is working things out together, realizing that you both play an equal part in your sexual communication.

Fifth, body language and spoken language are both vital in sexual expression. The previous chart hints at the key components. Keep in mind that sexual assertiveness is much more than the words you use. Perhaps here, more so than in other types of situations, body language is vital!

Sample Sexual Situations Calling for Assertiveness

Here are a couple of examples to help you understand each type of sexual communication better, including a "typical" response for each type.

Bedroom Boredom

During the past six months your partner has become less sexually attentive. You've been having intercourse less often, and your partner is not as enthusiastic or caring when you do. You've tried hard to provide motivation, but to no avail. Your frustration leads you to try this:

(a) You decide to be more patient. It crosses your mind that you are not sexy enough. You try being more attentive to your partner's every need.

(b) You tell your partner that you went to the doctor and were told that your hormone levels are low. You hint that more intercourse would be helpful.

(c) You lash out irrationally. Your feelings of upset have built to a boiling point. This evening's dull sexual encounter was the "last straw." Your partner retaliates. The verbal explosion lasts for hours. You are still seething and spend the night on the couch and the next week sulking.

(d) You tell your partner that your patience is exhausted, and that there must be a change in your sexual relationship. Your style is firm, but non-inflammatory. You suggest alternatives: a new self-help book you've read about; a weekend workshop conducted by a sex therapist; an appointment for relationship counseling. Your partner is reluctant, replying, "You go; it's your problem." You persist, cknowledging that some of the difficulty lies with you, pointing out that it affects you both. You repeat your desire that you both work on the problem.

Alcohol Amor

Your partner routinely drinks too much before you have intercourse. You feel that the drinking interferes with the quality of sex, and that it's time to take action:

(a) You hesitantly ask if there is "any chance that you might be drinking a little too much before intercourse?" Your partner is offended and responds defensively, "It's just normal social drinking."

(b) You begin talking about the "evils of alcohol" to others in front of your partner at social gatherings. At home you "misplace" the alcohol; when you do serve drinks, you "accidentally" drop your partner's drink.

(c) In the middle of intercourse you yell out, "You're a drunken slob!", dramatically pull away, and storm off to sleep on the couch.

(d) Speaking directly to your partner at a relatively calm private moment, you express your concern that the drinking before intercourse is interfering with the quality of sex for you. You give more details in a straightforward way, emphasizing that your relationship together is very important to you.

Some Basic Skill Areas of Assertive Sexuality

There is a basic landscape of sexual communication, key situations that repeatedly arise in relationships. Here are several, along with a few suggested "words of wisdom" which you may find useful.

Saying No.   Because of the sensitive nature of sexual communication, it doesn't hurt to use a little empathy and understanding in the process of saying no.

"I am not trying to hurt your feelings, but no. I don't want to do that."

"I love you, but I am really too tired tonight. How about tomorrow night?"

Saying Yes. We all like a little enthusiasm, especially when we propose something amorous!

"Sure. I'll go for that!"

"That sounds neat. Yes."

"Yes, let's have intercourse tonight."

Being Playful. Breaking New Ground. Why should sex be dull and boring, or the same all the time. Why not take risks, explore with each other, try something new? We need a freer, more imaginative and playful approach to sexuality.

"Honey, I've been reading this new book and I'd sure like to try position number 85 tonight."

"How about a massage with almond oil? We'll even light some incense!"

"Let's only kiss and fondle tonight. No intercourse."

Listening. The above situations involve speaking out. The other side, listening, is a lost art — especially when it comes to close, personal, intimate relationships. Take time actually to *hear* what your partner is saying.

Marital therapists often assign homework to help couples improve their listening skills. For example, try repeating back what your partner says and getting confirmation that you have heard the message correctly before you reply. Then have your partner do the same thing: fully, accurately listen to you before replying. It certainly can help you to feel heard and valued!

Negotiating/Compromising. These are skills that are helpful in all aspects of marriage or relationship. Learning to give and take, to let it be known what you desire, to take turns, are all necessary in assertive sexuality.

Singles Sexuality

Times are changing in singles sexual expression. Single persons seem to be headed in the same direction as their married peers: toward lasting relationships. Some experts feel that singles have burned out on casual encounters for two primary reasons: first, because they too desire intimacy and commitment; and second, because of the present scares regarding AIDS and herpes. Whatever the reasons, sexual conservatism seems to have replaced swinging as the vogue.

Sexual expression for singles is taking two paths. Many are living together and feel some degree of commitment.

Others are shifting back to the "no pre-marital sexual intercourse" stance. In either case, we feel that the ideas expressed above concerning assertive sexual expression apply.

Effective sexual communication is important whether or not formal vows are taken. The sooner you start on a course of mutual, honest and open sharing, the better you will feel.

Commitment

For many folks, the word *commitment* calls up an image of passivity: the style of the Victorians; the hang-in-there-against-all-odds approach; quiet devotion no matter what transpires. Well, things have changed.

Today's commitment is born in and grows out of active engagement with your partner. This new commitment results in steadfastness based on open communication. Commitment is an active, changing process, not a passive, changeless quality. Commitment requires partners to confront each other at times. Commitment understands that there will be rough times and negative forces deal with.

> Commitment is not determined silence.
> Commitment is not doggedly accepting every fault.
> Commitment is not dull.
> Commitment is not blind faith.
> Commitment is not ignorant.
> Commitment is not passive.
> Commitment is not standing still.
> Commitment is not naive.
> Commitment is not whimsical.
> Commitment is not oneness.

> Commitment is active.
> Commitment is striving.
> Commitment is communicating.
> Commitment is growing.

Commitment is engaging.
Commitment is encountering.
Commitment is joyfully alive.
Commitment is vibrant.
Commitment is dynamic.
Commitment is shared responsibility.

Commitment is intolerant of one-sided sexual idiosyncrasies, of sadistic treatment, of emotional traumatization. Commitment does not allow, and summarily curbs, physical or sexual abuse or assault. There are times to speak out forcefully and draw the line. Commitment does have limits.

As couples grow together, they also come to the realization that part of commitment is acceptance of (tolerable) conditions that will not change. Often this is a difficult realization. For years you may have convinced yourselves that you were open and accepting of each other's habits and faults that were not changing. But in the deeper recesses of your hearts remained a pocket of hope. Hope that someday your partner would be willing to have intercourse more frequently, or snuggle and cuddle and caress more, or dress more sexily, or not quickly turn over and fall asleep after intercourse.

Even though higher levels of commitment and devotion come from working out joys and concerns together over time, there are going to be some uncomfortable realities. No matter how loving and supportive and understanding and helpful you are, sometimes an annoying habit, an irritating mannerism, simply will not change.

As the wedding ring is a complete circle, so are we led back to the truth of the vows we little understood. We did not realize that "in sickness and in health" meant far more. Acceptance is the beginning of true love and the ending of ego. It is true intimacy.

We have often pointed out in this book that genuine assertiveness is a means for establishing equality in a relationship, not simply for expressing your own needs. Nowhere does that fact have more direct application than in the intimate realm of sexual relationships. In a relationship characterized by equality, love, intimacy, honest assertive expression, and commitment, the sexual dimension can grow to immense mutual satisfaction. Without those qualities, a fulfilling sexual relationship is unlikely.

18

Helping Others Live With the New Assertive You

All paths lead to the same goal: to convey to others what we are.

— Pablo Neruda

As you have grown in your own assertiveness, you have noticed changes in those around you. Your family, friends, co-workers, and others may have found it strange to notice that you have changed, and they may not be altogether happy about it.

Most folks like to be able to predict how others will act in a given situation...

"Mom's not going to like that!"
"You'll really get it when your father gets home!"
"The boss is going to hit the ceiling!"
"Jim will really be pleased."

...and usually will express surprise if their expectations are not met...

"Why is Mary acting so differently these days?"
"What's gotten into George?"
"It's not like you to say something like that."
"You never used to mind if I borrowed your...!"

Your growing assertiveness will have some direct effects upon those closest to you. They may be glad to see you behaving more effectively; however, they may find it uncomfortable that you have begun to "talk back," or to deny them full control in certain situations. You can prepare them for the changes in you; it will make a difference in how well they will support you in your growth.

How Does It Look From Outside?

"What's going on with Harold recently? He's been acting very strangely. I asked him if I could borrow his car, and he actually said no!*"*

People will notice. They'll wonder why you are no longer a pushover, or a grump. Some will applaud the changes, others will decry them — but they'll notice.

It's common for students of assertiveness to overdo it at first. That makes the changes even more noticeable. Others may see you as suddenly *aggressive*, and you may be. If you are saying "no" for the first time in your life, you may get a kick out of really belting it out. "NO — and don't ask me again!"

If you overreact like that, and "flaunt" your newfound self-expression, others will resent it. Not only are you no longer predictable, you are a royal pain in the neck! From the point of view of your friends and family, you may appear to be a pushy so-and-so — one they'd just as soon would go away.

If instead, you are too tentative about your assertions, others may notice that something is changed, but not realize what you are trying to do.

It may be a good idea to let those closest to you know what you are trying to do — at least those you can trust — and perhaps even to ask them for help. Becoming assertive will involve your friends eventually if you are successful — there is no reason to hide it from those who could help you along the way. More on this later in the chapter.

73

Be Aware of Your Impact on Others

You will need to develop some sensitivity to the reactions of others to your assertion. You can teach yourself to observe the effects and to watch for the subtle clues others will give to their reactions.

Many of the same non-verbal behaviors we have stressed in assertive expression are involved. You've learned to pay attention to your own eye contact, posture, gestures, facial expression, voice, distance.... Tune in to the same characteristics in your listeners, to help you know how you are coming across, and how they are responding.

Potential Adverse Reactions

In our experience with helping others to learn assertiveness for nearly two decades, we have found few negative results. Certain people do, however, respond in a disagreeable manner when they face assertion. Therefore, even if the assertion is handled properly — neither nonassertively nor aggressively to any degree — one may at times be faced with unpleasant reactions.

Here are a few examples:

Backbiting. After you have asserted yourself, the other person involved may be somewhat disgruntled, though perhaps not openly. For example, if you see someone jumping in line ahead of you and you respond assertively, the person may go to the end of the line, but grumble while passing you. You may hear such things as "Who do you think you are, anyway?" "Big deal!" "Big man!" and so forth. We think the best solution is simply to ignore the childish behavior. If you do retort in some manner, you are likely only to complicate the situation by acknowledging that the words "got to you."

Aggression. At times the other party may become outwardly hostile toward you. Yelling or screaming could be involved, or physical reactions like bumping, shoving, or hitting. Again, the best approach is to avoid escalating the condition. You may choose to express regret that she is upset by your actions, but remain steadfast in your assertion. This is especially true if you will have further contacts. If you back down on your assertion, you will simply reward this negative reaction. After such reinforcement, the next time you assert yourself with this person, the probability will be high that you will receive another aggressive reaction.

Temper Tantrums. In certain situations, you may assert yourself with someone who is used to being in charge. Such a person may react to your assertion by looking hurt, claiming precarious health, saying "You don't like me!" crying, feeling sorry for himself, or otherwise attempting to control you or make you feel guilty. Again, you must choose, but it is nearly always best to ignore such behavior.

Psychosomatic Reactions. Actual physical illness may occur in some individuals if you thwart a long-established habit. Abdominal pains, headaches, and feeling faint are just a few of the symptoms possible. Choose to be firm in the assertion, recognizing that the other person will adjust to the new situation in a short time. Be sure to be consistent in your assertion whenever the same situation recurs with this individual. If you are inconsistent, the other person may become confused and may eventually just ignore your assertions.

Overapologizing. On rare occasions after you have asserted yourself, the other party involved will be overly apologetic or humble to you. You should point out that such behavior is unnecessary. If, in later encounters she seems to be afraid of you or deferent toward you, do not take advantage. You could help to develop assertiveness in such a person, using the methods you have learned in this book.

Revenge. If you have a continuing relationship with someone with whom you have asserted yourself, that person may seek revenge. At first, it might be difficult to understand what is being attempted; but as time goes on the taunts may become quite evident. Once you are certain that someone is trying to make your life miserable, take steps to squelch the actions immediately. A recommended method is to directly confront the situation. Usually this is enough to get vengeful tactics to cease.

How Can You Include Others In Your Learning Process?

We suggested earlier in this chapter that you consider involving your most trusted friend(s) in your work on assertiveness. Try these steps:

...Tell your closest friend — be sure this is someone you can trust — that you are learning to be more assertive.

...Keep in mind that you will need to be careful when telling certain people about your attempts to become assertive. Those who have *your* best interests at heart will be supportive. Others — even some close friends and intimates — may actually undermine your efforts. Choose carefully.

...Tell your friend something about what it means to you to be assertive, and the differences between assertion and aggression.

...Ask your friend if she will help you.

...If she agrees, decide together on some specific behaviors she can watch for, and ask her to give you periodic feedback on how you are doing in those specifics — particularly the non-verbal components of behavior (Chapter 6).

...Recognize that sometimes your assertiveness will lead you to say "no" to your friend, or otherwise say or do something against *her* preferences. Discuss that with her in advance and as it occurs.

...Avoid announcing, "I'm going to be assertive now!" — as if that excuses rudeness or other inappropriate behavior, or allows you to avoid responsibility for your actions.

...If you are developing your assertiveness as a part of some form of therapy, you need not disclose that to anyone. Simply talk about your goals, and point out that you are learning from this book.

...If you are working with a therapist or other trainer, you may wish to bring your friend in for an orientation/training session.

...If you decide to go ahead and let a friend in on your plans, you may find the following statement useful in orienting that person to the assertiveness training process. Feel free to copy it, so long as you include the credit line at the bottom.

HOW A FRIEND CAN HELP...

Someone has trusted you enough to ask for your help.

A friend, relative, roommate, coworker, lover or "significant other" has asked you to read this brief statement because he or she has decided to make some changes. The process your friend is pursuing is called "assertiveness training" (AT), and its purpose is to help folks become more capable in expressing themselves.

Assertiveness is often confused with aggressiveness, so let's clear that up right now. Learning to be more *assertive* does not mean learning to push other folks around in order to get your way. It does mean standing up for yourself, expressing feelings directly and firmly, establishing equal relationships which take the needs of *both* people into account.

Your friend may be reading a book, taking a class, working with a counselor, practicing alone or in a group — there are lots of ways AT can be effective. It may take a few weeks, or even a few months, but you'll begin to notice some changes. Your friend may be expressing opinions about where to go out to eat, what's wrong with the government, how you clean up your half of the apartment... maybe saying "no" when you ask a favor... taking more initiative in conversation... giving more compliments than before... or even showing anger once in a while.

Not to worry. If these new actions were intended to threaten *you*, your friend would not have asked you to read this!

Most people find that increased assertiveness makes folks even more pleasant to be around. They're more spontaneous, less inhibited, more honest and direct, feel better about themselves, maybe even healthier!

So... how do *you* figure into this?

Well, your friend has asked you to read this so you'll know a little about what's going on in her or his life right now, and better understand the changes you may be seeing in the coming weeks and months.

You are evidently a trusted person in your friend's life, because it can be risky to let someone know about changes one plans to make. Sort of like telling people about your dreams, or your New Year's Resolutions. If things don't work out, the person is vulnerable to some real hurt.

Please honor the trust that has been extended to you.

Here are some ways you can help...

...find out something about how your friend hopes to change, so you'll know what to look for.

...when you see the desired changes — however small — give him a "pat on the back."

...be honest in your own dealings with your friend... including pointing out when she "goes overboard" trying to be assertive.

...read up on assertiveness yourself.

...actively "coach" your friend with specific behavior changes, such as improved eye contact or voice tone.

...be a good model of assertiveness yourself.

...help your friend "rehearse" special situations, such as job interviews, or confrontations.

You'll likely find your thoughtfulness repaid manyfold. You may find yourself learning a thing or two in the process!

*   *   *   *   *

From *Your Perfect Right: A Guide to Assertive Living* (Fifth Edition). Copyright 1986, by Robert E. Alberti and Michael L. Emmons. Reprinted with permission of Impact Publishers, San Luis Obispo, CA 93406.

19

Beyond Assertiveness

God, give us the serenity to accept what cannot be changed, the courage to change what should be changed, and the wisdom to distinguish one from the other.

— Reinhold Niebuhr

Our theme throughout this book has been to emphasize *individual choice,* and the value of assertive behavior to people seeking self-direction. The perceptive reader will have recognized some of the potential shortcomings and hazards inherent in personal assertiveness. Sensitivity is required in taking into account some of these limitations and potentially negative consequences of asserting yourself.

Although assertive behavior will most often be its own reward, the consequences on occasion may deflate its value. Consider, for example, the young boy who assertively refuses the big bully's request to ride his new bike, and as a result finds himself nursing a black eye! His assertion was perfectly legitimate, but the other person was unwilling to accept the denial of his desire. Therefore, without suggesting that assertiveness be avoided if it appears hazardous, we do encourage you to consider the probable *consequences* of your assertive acts. Under certain circumstances, the value of an assertion will be outweighed by the value of avoiding the probable response!

Sometimes with adults the reaction is more subtle than that of the street bully. Arlene found herself alienated from friends of twenty years when she criticized the way they were "spoiling" their son. It was nearly a year before the wound was healed. Meanwhile, Arlene wondered if the assertion really had been worth it.

If you *know how to* act assertively, you are free to *choose* whether or not you will. If you are *unable* to act assertively, you have no choices; you will be governed by others, and your well-being will suffer. *Our most important goal for this book is to enable YOU to make the choice!*

Choosing Not to Assert Yourself

It's worth repeating: *Choice* is the key word in the assertion process. As long as you know in your own mind (from previous, successful assertive encounters) that you *can* assert yourself, you may decide not to do so in a given instance. Following are some circumstances where one may *choose* nonassertiveness:

Overly Sensitive Individuals. On occasion, from your own observations, you may conclude that a certain person is unable to accept even the slightest assertion. When this is apparent, it is better to resign yourself to this fact rather than risk the consequences. Although there are those who fake weakness as a means to manipulate others, certain individuals are so easily threatened that the slightest disagreement causes them to withdraw inwardly (thus hurting themselves) or explode outwardly (thus hurting others). If you must be around someone like this, it is possible to build up your own tolerance, accept the person, and put up with the situation.

Redundancy. Once in a while, a person who has taken advantage of you will realize what's happened — before you get a chance to express yourself — and then remedy the situation in an appropriate way. It is not appropriate to *then* pipe up and assert yourself. Don't wait a long time *wishing*

that the other person will notice. Nevertheless, don't hesitate
to be assertive if the offender fails to make the amends which
you feel should reasonably be made.
Being Understanding. Now and then you may choose not to be
assertive because you notice that the person is having
difficulty; there can be extenuating circumstances. At a
restaurant one evening it was evident that the new cook was
having great difficulty with everything. When the meal
arrived not exactly as ordered, we chose not to be assertive
rather than hassle him further.

When someone you know is having an "off" day and is in
a rare bad mood, you may *choose* to overlook things that may
be going wrong between you, or postpone a confrontation to a
more productive time. *Caution:* It is easy to use "not wanting
to hurt the other's feelings" as a rationalization for
nonassertiveness when assertion would be more appropriate.
If you find yourself doing this more than occasionally, we
suggest that you carefully examine your real motives.
Manipulators and Incorrigible People. In everyone's life there
are those who are just plain difficult! Your best efforts at
appropriate assertion with such a person may result in an
undesired reaction nearly all the time. Some people are so
unpleasant that it is simply not worth it to confront them. And
sometimes the potential gain is not worth the price one must
pay in personal pain. We support your *choice* not to assert
yourself in such circumstances. Nevertheless, we once again
urge you to examine any such situation very carefully;
consider the possibility that you may be using "not worth it"
as an excuse not to confront a difficult-but-not-impossible
situation!

When You Are Wrong

Especially in your early assertions, you may assert
yourself when you have incorrectly interpreted a situation.
Also, you may assert yourself with poor technique and offend
the other person. If either of these situations does occur, be

very willing to say that you have been wrong. There is no need to get carried away in making amends, of course; but be open enough to indicate that you know when you have been mistaken. And don't hesitate to be assertive with that person in the future when the situation calls for it.

"It's Too Late Now!"

We are often asked about past situations by people who feel they can do nothing about a problem which happened some time ago. Frustrated by the consequences of their earlier lack of assertion, they nevertheless feel helpless to change the situation now.

Charlene, a busy executive, often completed letters and reports late in the day, and wound up asking George, her secretary, to stay late so he could type and duplicate the work for meetings the following morning. The first time, George assumed that the request was due to unique circumstances at that time. He willingly agreed to help out. Later, he found the "special request" had become an *expectation,* and occurred two or three times a week. Although he enjoyed the work, it interfered with his personal life, and he began to think of quitting the job.

George sought help in an assertiveness training group, where he somewhat tentatively brought the situation up for discussion. He found the trainer and group members very supportive. Selecting a relatively assertive woman in the group, he "rehearsed" with her a scene in which he confronted Charlene with his feelings. He did poorly at first, apologizing and allowing the "boss" to convince him that such "loyalty to the company" was necessary to the job. With feedback and support from the group, however, George improved his ability to express his feelings effectively and not be cowed by the executive's response.

The next day, George confronted Charlene at the office, made his point, and arranged a more reasonable schedule for such projects. In the two months that followed, she made "special requests" only twice, and only when the circumstances clearly *were* unusual. Both were pleased with the result.

The point of this discussion is that it is seldom too late for an appropriate assertion, even if a situation has grown worse over some time. Approaching the person involved — yes, even a family member, spouse, lover, boss, employee — with an honest "I've been concerned about... for some time" or "I've been wanting to talk with you about..." can lead to a most productive effort at resolution of an uncomfortable issue. And it can encourage open and honest communication in the future.

Keep in mind the importance of stating your feelings in such a way as to accept responsibility for them: "I'm concerned..." *not* "You've made me upset..."; "I'm mad..." *not* "You make me mad..."

Another important reason to go back and take care of old business with others is that unfinished business continues to gnaw away at you. Resentment from experiences which created anger or hurt won't just go away. Such feelings result in a widening gap between people, and the resulting mistrust and potential grudge are hurtful to both persons.

Even if the old issues cannot be amicably resolved, doing all you can to *attempt* reconciliation is a very healthy and worthwhile step for you. We recognize that opening up old wounds can be painful. And there are certain risks — the outcomes *could* be worse than before. Despite these risks, we have seen so many people gain great rewards from resolving old conflicts that we do not hesitate to encourage you to do all *you* can to work out any such problems in your own life.

One more point: As we have cautioned before, do not attempt to *begin* your journey toward new assertiveness with highly risky relationships — those which are *very* important to you. This is a rather advanced step, and should come after you have mastered the basics.

The Swing Of the Pendulum

A question that often arises from the audience when we speak on assertiveness:

"I have this friend who went through assertion training and now is unbearable! This person, who used to be peaceful and quiet, is complaining about everything. She has really gone overboard! Isn't assertion training dangerous at times because it creates monsters?"

People who have considered themselves underdogs throughout life, and then learned to be assertive, do often move beyond assertion into verbal aggressiveness. The message may be, "Now I've got my chance, and I'll set a few people straight!" Feelings held down or covered up for so many years often come out with a "bang" when new skills for self-expression are learned.

The converse of this situation may also be true: Those who have been prone to aggressive behavior, such as manipulating, may go overboard when first learning assertion, becoming overly sensitive and responsive to people. It can be flabbergasting to suddenly be treated like a queen or king by someone who was formerly derisive and calculating!

Both of these dramatic shifts in behavior are normal reactions and to be expected under the circumstances. The pendulum was "stuck." Now released, the person seeks to experience the full range of behavior. We suggest patience in these instances. The pendulum will swing back after a relatively brief period of experimentation, and assertion will be accepted eventually as the best alternative.

Assertiveness in a Holistic Perspective

Proponents of various systems of therapy generally overemphasize their particular brand of help and exclude other valuable approaches. We psychologists, for example, often neglect to look beyond mental treatments for the problems of clients. However, there is never just one cure for all that ails us.

Assertiveness training is an extremely valuable tool for gaining self-confidence and self-control in life, but it is by no means a cure-all. AT works best when used along with other psychological, physical, and spiritual approaches. We espouse a holistic-eclectic treatment system, integrating a variety of psychological methods with physical and spiritual considerations.

The human mental, physical, and spiritual dimensions are inseparable. It is vital to deal with each person as a total being.

If you are undertaking an analysis of your own psychological functioning, take a careful look at the physical and spiritual areas as well. Medical history, current medical condition, dietary and physical exercise patterns, spiritual strengths and weaknesses — are all important considerations in a thorough assessment of well-being. Do not assume that a lack of assertiveness, for example, will be adequately dealt with by an AT program alone. The problem could be largely dietary! Examine all the possibilities, and engage medical and/or spiritual as well as psychological professionals if you need their help.

The idea of "holistic health" is something of a fad in our society now, yet the historic roots of holistic procedures are traceable to ancient Egypt. The modern regeneration of these concepts has been stimulated by such factors as increased consumer activism, exhorbitant health care costs, the women's movement, and the assertiveness movement. Despite the continuing tendency for specialization, an increasingly holistic outlook is emerging among health professionals in all fields.

To help place assertiveness in a holistic perspective, then, let us identify those principles of holistic health which are now generally agreed upon among holistic practitioners: (1) Holistic health emphasizes psychological, physical and spiritual wellness; (2) Responsibility for health lies with each individual; (3) Health must be viewed within the context of one's family, community, and culture; (4) No single health system has a monopoly on "truth"; (5) Natural, drugless procedures are to be preferred whenever possible; (6) Total health is dependent upon the curative power of the body, and the inner power of the spirit; (7) Health is a lifelong process involving prevention and cure of illness, maintenance of health, and striving toward optimum well-being.

Should you wish more information regarding holistic treatment methods, we suggest the following material (see the Bibliography): Emmons (1978); Hastings, et al. (1980); Pelletier (1979); Ulene (1977).

We urge you to develop an assertive lifestyle, and to take care of yourself, holistically!

Assertiveness and Common Sense

We've emphasized action in this book. When we first began to do assertiveness training back in the late 1960s, we found it an effective procedure for our clients who had difficulty expressing themselves. Most of them were shy, nonassertive, reluctant to take any action on their own behalf. For them, it seemed the most effective approach was to *activate* them, to get them going again, to teach them to "stand up, speak out, and talk back."

Later we came to recognize that many people were using the idea of taking such action as a license to act aggressively, or at least foolishly. Some trainers were advocating — as homework in assertiveness — that people go into restaurants and ask just for a glass of water. Or into service stations and ask just to have the windows washed (in those days service stations actually did that sort of thing!).

Let us put in a plea, then, for common sense:

Don't Manipulate. Assertiveness goes a long way, when used appropriately. But it ought not be used as a tool for manipulation, or as a means to "get your way" at the expense of others (aggressive), or as a constant style of behavior.

Don't Get In A Rut. You need not "assert yourself" all the time. How boring, — and boorish — to go about always making yourself heard, always speaking out. Make assertiveness *one tool* in your repertoire of behaviors, one way to act which you can use when it is important and needed. Nothing is good all the time! There is such a thing as "too much of a good thing!"

Be Kind. Kindness is a word we don't hear enough these days. Somehow it has fallen out of fashion. It has been our intent since the beginning of our work with assertiveness to help humans treat each other with respect, thoughtfulness, and yes, kindness. The idea of assertiveness for those who had been "pushed around" earlier was to help them gain the respect that they had been missing from others.

Assertiveness is *not* incompatible with kindness, thoughtfulness, compassion, empathy, politeness. A truly assertive lifestyle is very concerned for others, and their rights. The term "empathic assertion" has been used to describe those forms of self-expression which are directly aimed at the needs of another person.

Be Yourself. An unfortunate number of people have interpreted assertiveness as a monolithic concept — as if there were one single definition which qualified a behavior as "assertive." We discussed this at some length in Chapter 4, but we'd like to underscore it here by encouraging recognition of individual differences.

Everybody has a unique view of the world; that is part of the joy of the human experience. Don't try to shape others into your image of them! Don't assume there is only one way to be assertive in a given circumstance! Let people choose to be non-assertive if they wish. Let there be "different strokes for different folks!"

Be Persistent — But Not A Pest. One of the most important but often overlooked aspects of assertive behavior is *persistence*. It is rarely enough just to ask for what you want.

You may need to ask again, to direct your request to someone in authority, to write a letter, to bring some pressure to bear from another source (a consumer advocacy group, a regulatory agency)....

Is your cause important? Go back again if you don't get help the first time. See the manager. Call the president of the company. Tell your neighbor again about his noisy dog. Remind your boss about the raise.

Remember to be assertive in your persistence — nagging can be aggressive!

Practice — But Don't Get "Perfect." Some types of so-called "assertive" responses can seem really mechanical and rehearsed. While we advocate that you rehearse while you are developing your style and skills in assertiveness, we consider it very important that you develop a *personal* style — integrating assertiveness with your own unique way of dealing with people. If you come off sounding like our book, or like someone else's "scripts for assertive situations" you'll lose credibility, and people will not take you seriously.

Shrinks Don't Fit. Don't try to "psychoanalyze" people! Some folks go around trying to "think psychologically," always figuring out how others are likely to react, and shaping their behavior by the way they believe it will affect others. It is rare that anyone — even those of us who are trained psychologists — is able to do that successfully.

Instead, try to be yourself, be assertive, and take others' needs, rights, and respect into account.

Membership in the Human Community

Thornton Wilder, in his popular play, *Our Town*, addressed one of his key characters thus: "Jane Crofeet, the Crofeet Farm, Grover's Corners, Sutton County, New Hampshire, United States of America, Continent of North America, the Earth, the Solar System, the Universe, the Mind of God." Wilder showed a remarkable sense of citizenship in the world; few of us have so thoughtfully considered our relationships to the entire human community.

Indeed, is it even possible to deal with that virtually unreachable concept? In what sense *am* I a world citizen? I can talk with and see my neighbors in the local community. I can visit, with minimal difficulty, people in nearby states, or even across the country, and, if I am fortunate, around the world. I can share government agencies; vote in local, state and national elections; share a historical and cultural heritage with other citizens of the United States. What have I in common with the people of Nepal, or Luxembourg, or Sri Lanka? Do I really think of them as my brothers and sisters in humankind?

No individual can exist alone. None of us has the necessary knowledge, skills, or personal resources necessary to function with total independence in the world. We are interdependent, and our assertiveness must take into account and respect our neighbors' needs as well as our own.

Even without the dramatic evidence offered from space, it's easy to see the fragility of world order in any day's headlines. We note the continuing efforts by governments of many nations to maintain world peace and some balance of order on the planet. And we see how easily aggression and the quest for power disturb that balance.

So many international issues remain unresolved, awaiting assertive action by those courageous enough to transcend nationalistic limits and assume leadership in *solving problems*, rather than displaying power. Hunger, extreme poverty, sanitation, disposal of nuclear and other hazardous wastes... the list goes on.

The principles of assertive action which we have discussed throughout this book apply to these concerns as well. Perhaps you have found assertiveness training helpful in your own life and relationships. We urge you to demonstrate your appreciation for that help by taking assertive action as a world citizen. Write letters supporting public officials who take courageous action. Contact your elected representatives to express your views on important issues.

Work to replace aggression with assertion wherever you can. You may choose to support tighter controls on handguns, for instance, or reduced television violence. Some will demonstrate against nuclear power plants or weapons proliferation. Perhaps you advocate free-enterprise replacement of government bureaucracies which fail to provide necessary services. The ERA may be your major cause. Support is always needed for local programs of rape crisis intervention, and training for parents to help them protect their children.

The principle of assertive action is well established in Western culture, and a vital element in the U.S. Constitution. The spirit of civil disobedience, when other attempts to change intolerable situations have failed, has a proud heritage. Henry David Thoreau is the "patron saint" of civil disobedience, but one need look no further than the U.S. Declaration of Independence or such famous historic events as the Boston Tea Party for other well known and highly respected foundations.

A vital principle of any such action, of course, is the individual's willingness to accept responsibility for the consequences thereof. Twentieth century examples of such personally responsible, public assertiveness are Mahatma Ghandi, Martin Luther King, Desmond Tutu, and Lech Walesa. Whatever our personal views of the substantive issues in their actions, we must stand in awe of those who have made their deepest beliefs public by living accordingly, caring more for the welfare of humankind than for their individual comfort and safety.

Ultimately, those acts which are in the best interest of our fellow humans are in our own best interests as well. If I act assertively to right a social wrong, I act to the benefit of all who are members of the society, including myself. Thus assertive action, in the best sense, is at once in my own self-interest *and* unselfish!

There are a thousand causes worthy of your energies. If your assertiveness ends when your steak is served the way you like it, or when you get correct change, your life may be more pleasant temporarily, but will not count for much.

Oliver Wendell Holmes put it in perspective (do forgive his sexist language):

"A man must share in the action and passion of his times, at the risk of being judged not to have lived

Beyond Assertiveness

Enough. The rest is up to you.

Keep in mind:

...Assertiveness, as other social behavior, is learned. You *can* change yourself if you wish to do so.

...Change is hard work. It usually comes slowly, and in small steps. Don't try to tackle too much at once. Succeed by taking *achievable* steps!

...There are no magic answers. While assertiveness doesn't always work (for us either!), it sure beats the alternatives — nearly all the time! Don't let failures at first stop you from trying again.

...Give yourself credit when you bring about changes in your life. Even the smallest accomplishments deserve a pat on the back!

...Don't hesitate to ask for help — including professional help when you need it. Everyone needs help at times.

...You are working with an infinitely valuable resource — yourself. Take good care!

You are unique, an individual, with your own size, shape, color, age, ethnic and cultural background, sex, lifestyle, education, ideas, values, occupation, relationships, thoughts, behavior patterns. In this book we have had to generalize a great deal. AT is not all things to all people. *You* must decide what is relevant for you. If you choose to use AT as a tool to help you become the person you want to be, you must also decide how to apply its principles to your own unique life situation.

Remember that assertiveness is *not* a tool for manipulation, or intimidation, or getting your way. It is a means to stand up for your own rights, to express your anger, to reach out to others, to build equal relationships, to express your affection, to be more direct. Most importantly, it is one means to become the person you want to be, to feel good about yourself, and to demonstrate your caring and respect for the rights of others.

Appendices

Appendix A

Practice Situations

The everyday life situations which follow call for assertive behavior, and cause difficulty for many people. Each situation is presented with alternatives from which you may choose a response. Each alternative response may be categorized in the "nonassertive-aggressive-assertive" framework we have described.

The situations are designed for your practice according to the step-by-step process described in Chapter 12. Select situations appropriate to your needs, and work slowly, on one item at a time. As you read the situation description, fill in the details from your own imagination.

Follow steps 4 to 7 of Chapter 12, utilizing the alternative responses suggested here for each situation, and any others you may think of. For each situation you choose, enact the role-playing and feedback exercises described in Steps 8, 9, 11 and 12; then continue with remaining steps of the step-by-step process.

The examples are grouped according to several characteristic types of situations: *family, consumer, employment, school and community,* and *social.* In each case, only a few situations are suggested, although the number of categories and examples is as infinite as life itself. We urge you to come up with more examples of your own to extend your practice.

Family Situations

Slumber Party. Your 12-year-old daughter is having a slumber party with five other girls. It is past 2 a.m.; the girls should have settled down to sleep by now, but they're still making a lot of noise.

Alternative Responses:

(a) You toss and turn in bed, wishing your spouse would get up and say something to the girls. You're really angry, but just lie there trying to block out the sounds.

(b) Jumping out of bed, you scold the girls angrily, especially your daughter, for their conduct.

(c) Talking to the girls in a firm tone, so they'll know you mean business, you tell them that you've had enough for tonight. You point out that you need to get up early tomorrow, and that everyone needs to get to sleep.

Late for Dinner. Your wife was supposed to be home for dinner right after work. Instead, she returns hours later explaining she was out with the girls for a few drinks. She is obviously drunk.

Alternative Responses:

(a) You say nothing about how thoughtless she has been, but simply start preparing something for her to eat.

(b) Screaming, yelling and crying, you tell her that she is a drunken fool, doesn't care about your feelings, is a poor example for the children. You ask about what the neighbors will think. You demand that she get her own dinner.

(c) You calmly and firmly let her know that she should have informed you beforehand that she was going out for a few drinks and would likely be late. Telling her that her cold dinner is in the kitchen, you add that you expect to discuss her behavior further tomorrow.

Visiting Relative. Aunt Margaret, with whom you prefer not to spend much time, is on the telephone. She has just told you of her plans to spend three weeks visiting you, beginning next week.

Alternative Responses:

(a) You think, "Oh, no!" but say, "We'd love to have you come and stay as long as you like!"

(b) You tell her the children have just come down with bad colds, and the spare bed has a broken spring and you'll be going to Cousin Bill's weekend after next — none of which is true.

(c) You say, "We'll be glad to have you come for the weekend, but we simply can't invite you for longer. A short visit is happier for everyone, and we'll want to see each other again sooner We have lots of school and community activities which take up most of our evenings after work."

Past Midnight. Your teenage son has just returned from a school party. It is 3 o'clock in the morning, and you have been frantic, concerned primarily for his well-being, since you had expected him home before midnight.

Alternative Responses:

(a) You turn over and go to sleep.

(b) You shout, "Where the hell have you been? Do you have any idea what time it is? You've kept me up all night! You thoughtless, inconsiderate, selfish, no-good bum — I ought to make you sleep in the street!"

(c) You say, "I've been very worried about you, son. You said you'd be home before midnight, and I've been frantic for hours. Are you alright? I wish you'd called me! Tomorrow we'll discuss your arrangements for staying out late."

Consumer Situations

Haircut. At the barber shop, the barber has just finished cutting your hair and turns the chair toward the mirror so you can inspect. You feel that

you would like the sides trimmed more.
Alternative Responses:
(a) You nod your head and say, "That's ok."
(b) Abruptly you demand that he do a more thorough job, adding sarcastically, "You sure didn't take much off the sides, did you?"
(c) You tell the barber you would like to have the sides trimmed more.

Short-changed. As you are leaving a store after a small purchase, you discover that you have been short-changed by three dollars.
Alternative Responses:
(a) Pausing for a moment, you try to decide if $3 is worth the effort. After a few moments, you decide it is not and go on your way.
(b) You hurry back into the store and loudly demand your money, making a derogatory comment about "cashiers who can't add."
(c) Re-entering the store, you catch the attention of the clerk, saying that you were short-changed by three dollars. In the process of explaining, you display the change you received back.

Waiting in Line. You are standing near a cash register waiting to pay for your purchase and have it wrapped. Others, who have come after you, are being waited on first. You are getting tired of waiting.
Alternative Responses:
(a) You give up and decide not to buy the article.
(b) Shouting, "You sure get poor service in this store!" you slam the intended purchase down on the counter and walk out.
(c) In a voice loud enough to be heard, you tell the clerk you were ahead of people who have already been served. You ask to be waited on now.

Phone Blues. You are at home, hoping for a restful day. The phone rings, and you answer to a voice stating your full name and asking if that is you. The call is long distance, so you feel it might be important. Then you hear. "This is Rocky Road Magazine. We are conducting a readership survey. Have you heard of our magazine?"
Alternative Responses:
(a) You are polite, don't interrupt and answer all of the caller's questions. Soon you hear a "sales pitch" instead of a readership survey. The call lasts ten minutes.
(b) You yell, "You people are a bunch of vultures! Don't you know anything about telephone privacy? Stick it in your ear!" You slam down the phone.
(c) You state firmly, "I am not interested." The caller replies, "I only want to ask you a few questions." You repeat firmly, "I am not interested." You hang up the phone.

Employment Situations

Working Late. You and your partner have an engagement this evening which has been planned for several weeks. You plan to leave immediately after work. During the day, however, your supervisor asks you to stay late this evening to work on a special assignment.

Alternative Responses:

(a) You say nothing about your important plans and simply agree to stay until the work is finished.

(b) In a nervous, abrupt voice you say, "No, I will not work late tonight!" Adding a brief criticism of the boss for not planning the work schedule better, you then turn back to your work.

(c) In a firm, pleasant voice, you explain your important plans and say you will not be able to stay this evening to work on the special assignment, but perhaps you can help find an alternative solution.

Deniable Passion. One of your co-workers has been making sexual overtures toward you. You are not the least bit interested and have begun to feel harassed.

Alternative Responses:

(a) You begin wearing clothing that is less appealing, change your hair style, and start looking down each time the person approaches.

(b) The next time the person makes an overture you state, "I hate your guts! You are scum! You are so ugly that Frankenstein wouldn't have you."

(c) After a recent incident, you sit and talk quietly with the person. You note that you are feeling pursued and do not wish to be, giving examples of what you mean. Finally you say that if the approaches do not stop, you will file a report with your employer.

Below Par. One of your employees has been doing sub-standard work recently. You decide it is best to deal with the situation before it gets out of control.

Alternative Responses:

(a) "I'm sorry to bring this up, but I know you must have a good reason why your work has seemed to slide a little lately."

(b) "Things between us are not right. You have been making me mad lately by doing a lousy job. If you don't shape up pronto, you will be out of here."

(c) "I am very concerned about your work performance recently. You won't be receiving a pay increase this period. Let's analyze what's been going on and see what improvements you can make for the future."

Job Error. You have made a mistake on the job. Your supervisor discovers it and is letting you know rather harshly that you should not have been so careless.

Alternative Responses:

(a) Overapologizing, you say, "I'm sorry. I was stupid. How silly of me. I'll never let it happen again!"

(b) You bristle up and say, "You have no business whatsoever criticizing my work. Leave me alone, and don't bother me in the future. I'm capable of handling my own job!"

(c) You agree that you made the mistake, saying, "It was my mistake. I will be more careful next time. However, I feel you are being somewhat harsh and I see no need for that."

Late to Work. One of your subordinates has been coming 'n late consistently for the last three or four days.

Alternative Responses:

(a) You grumble to yourself or to others about the situation, but say nothing to the person, hoping he will start coming in early.

(b) You tell the worker off, indicating that he has no right to take advantage of you and that he had better get to work on time or else you will see that he is fired.

(c) You point out to the worker that you have observed him coming in late recently and wonder, "Is there an explanation I should know about? You'll have to start coming to work on time. You should have come to me and explained the situation, rather than saying nothing at all, and leaving me up in the air."

School and Community Situations

Quiet Prof. In a lecture with 300 students, the professor speaks softly and you know that many others are having trouble hearing him as you are.

Alternative Responses:

(a) You continue to strain to hear, eventually moving closer to the front of the room, but say nothing about his too-soft voice.

(b) You yell out, "Speak up!"

(c) You raise your hand, get the professor's attention and ask if he would please speak louder.

Clarification. At a Lion's Club meeting, the President is discussing the procedures for the annual high school speech contest. You are puzzled by several of his statements and believe he has incorrectly described the rules.

Alternative Responses:

(a) You say nothing, but continue to puzzle over the question, looking up your notes from last year's contest later in the day.

(b) You interrupt, telling him he is wrong, pointing out the mistake and correcting him from your own knowledge of the contest. Your tone is derisive, and your choice of words obviously makes him ill-at-ease.

(c) You ask the President to further explain the procedures, expressing your confusion and noting the source of your conflicting information.

Morals. You are one of eleven people in a discussion group on human sexuality. The concepts being supported by three or four of the more verbal students are contrary to your personal moral code.

Alternative Responses:

(a) You listen quietly, not disagreeing openly with the other members or describing your own views.

(b) You loudly denounce the views which have been expressed. Your defense of your own beliefs is strong, and you urge others to accept your point of view as the only correct one.

(c) You speak up in support of your own beliefs, identifying yourself with an apparently unpopular position, but not disparaging the beliefs of others in the group.

Know It All. As a member of the community beautification committee, you are dismayed by the continued dominance of group discussion by Ms. Brown, an opinionated member who has "the answer" to every question. She has begun another tirade. As usual, no one has said anything about it after several minutes.

Alternative Responses:

(a) Your irritation increases, but you remain silent.

(b) You explode verbally, curse Ms. Brown for "not giving anyone else a chance," and declare her ideas out-of-date and worthless.

(c) You interrupt, saying, "Excuse me, Ms. Brown." When recognized, you express your personal irritation about Ms. Brown's monopoly on the group's time. Speaking directly to her as well as the other group members, you suggest a discussion procedure which will permit all members an opportunity to take part, and will minimize dominance by a single individual.

Social Situations

Breaking the Ice. At a party where you don't know anyone except the host, you want to circulate and get to know others. You walk up to three people talking.

Alternative Responses:

(a) You stand close to them and smile but say nothing, waiting for them to notice you.

(b) You listen to the subject they are talking about, then break in and disagree with someone's viewpoint.

(c) You break into the conversation and introduce yourself.

(d) You wait for a pause in the conversation, then introduce yourself and ask if you may join in.

Making a Date. You'd like to ask out a person you have met and talked with three or four times recently.
Alternative Responses:
(a) You sit around the telephone going over in your mind what you will say and how your friend will respond. Several times you lift the phone and are almost finished dialing, then hang up.
(b) You phone and as soon as your friend answers, you respond by saying, "Hi, baby, we're going out together this weekend!" Seemingly taken aback, your friend asks who is calling.
(c) You call, and when your friend answers, you say who is calling and ask how school (job, etc.) is going. The reply is, "Fine, except I am worried about a test I will be taking soon." Following the lead, you talk for a few minutes about the test. Then you say that you would like to go together to a show on Friday evening.

Smoke Gets in Your Lungs. You are at a public meeting in a large room. A man enters the room and sits down next to you, puffing enthusiastically on a large cigar. The smoke is very offensive to you.
Alternative Responses:
(a) You suffer the offensive smoke in silence, deciding it is the right of the other person to smoke if he wishes.
(b) You become very angry, demand that he move or put out the cigar and loudly assail the evils and health hazards of the smoking habit.
(c) You firmly but politely ask him to refrain from smoking because it is offensive to you.
(d) You ask him to sit in another seat if he prefers to continue smoking, since you were there first.

Family Situations

Holy Terror. Your son's pre-school teacher tells you he is hitting the other children. At home he "runs the show," staying up late, roughing up the pets, not eating properly. In the past you have thought his behavior "cute."
Alternative Responses:
(a) You talk gently to your son about not hitting the other children. He says the other kids are mean, but that he is sorry. He jumps in your lap and you say, "You are such a sweet boy, I love you."
(b) You grab your son roughly and say that if he hits anyone else that you will beat his bottom till it is raw.
(c) After discussing the issue with the teacher and ruling out any physical causes, you sign up the entire family for counseling.

Plastic Money. Finances are tight. When you receive the credit card bill for the month, you are shocked. Your spouse has charges that seem excessive and unnecessary.

Alternative Responses:

(a) You go to the bank and cash a check for an equal amount of money. After spending it, you feel that you have gained your revenge. You don't mention the credit card.

(b) You realize that you also have over-spent before. You still feel upset, but decide to be understanding this time.

(c) You arrange an appropriate time to discuss the finances, and tell your partner that when you opened the statement, you were shocked at the charges. Asking your spouse for an explanation, you also express your wish to establish agreeable guidelines for the use of the credit card.

Sagging Sex. During the past six months, your spouse has not been sexually attentive. You're having intercourse less often, and your spouse is not as enthusiastic or caring. You have tried harder to motivate your partner, but to no avail.

(a) You decide that two can play this game. You withdraw, complain to your friends, and criticize your spouse openly in front of the children about non-related matters.

(b) The feelings of upset have built to a boiling point. One evening, after another dull sexual encounter, you lash out irrationally. Your spouse retaliates. The verbal explosion lasts for hours. Still seething, you spend that night on the couch and the next week sulking.

(c) In a non-inflammatory, but firm style, you speak to your partner honestly and openly about your feelings. You suggest that you both take part in a couple's workshop or go see a counselor to work on the problem.

Appendix B

Universal Declaration of Human Rights

WHEREAS recognition of the inherent dignity and of the equal and inalienable rights of all members of the human family is the foundation of freedom, justice and peace in the world,

WHEREAS disregard and contempt for human rights have resulted in barbarous acts which have outraged the conscience of mankind, and the advent of a world in which human beings shall enjoy freedom of speech and belief and freedom from fear and want has been proclaimed as the highest aspiration of the common people,

WHEREAS, it is essential, if man is not to be compelled to have recourse, as a last resort, to rebellion against tyranny and oppression, that human rights should be protected by the rule of law,

WHEREAS it is essential to promote the development of friendly relations between nations,

WHEREAS the peoples of the United Nations have in their Charter reaffirmed their faith in fundamental human rights, in the dignity and worth of the human person and in the equal rights of men and women and have determined to promote social progress and better standards of life in larger freedom,

WHEREAS Member States have pledged themselves to achieve, in co-operation with the United Nations, the promotion of universal respect for and observance of human rights and fundamental freedoms,

WHEREAS a common understanding of these rights and freedoms is of the greatest importance for the full realization of this pledge,

NOW, THEREFORE, THE GENERAL ASSEMBLY PROCLAIMS this Universal Declaration of Human Rights as a common standard of achievement for all peoples and all nations, to the end that every individual and every organ of society, keeping this Declaration constantly in mind, shall strive by teaching and education to promote respect for these rights and freedoms and by progressive measures, national and international, to secure their universal and effective recognition and observance, both among the peoples of Member States themselves and among the peoples of territories under their jurisdiction.

Article 1. All human beings are born free and equal in dignity and rights. They are endowed with reason and conscience and should act towards one another in a spirit of brotherhood.

Article 2. Everyone is entitled to all the rights and freedoms set forth in this Declaration, without distinction of any kind, such as race, colour, sex, language, religion, political or other opinion, national or social origin, property, birth or other status.

Furthermore, no distinction shall be made on the basis of the political, jurisdictional or international status of the country or territory to which a person belongs, whether it be independent, trust, non-self-governing or under any other limitation of sovereignty.

Article 3. Everyone has the right to life, liberty and security of person.

Article 4. No one shall be held in slavery or servitude; slavery and the slave trade shall be prohibited in all their forms.

Article 5. No one shall be subjected to torture or to cruel, inhuman or degrading treatment or punishment.

Article 6. Everyone has the right to recognition everywhere as a person before the law.

Article 7. All are equal before the law and are entitled without any discrimination to equal protection of the law. All are entitled to equal protection against any discrimination in violation of this Declaration and against any incitement to such discrimination.

Article 8. Everyone has the right to an effective remedy by the competent national tribunals for acts violating the fundamental rights granted him by the constitution or by law.

Article 9. No one shall be subjected to arbitrary arrest, detention of exile.

Article 10. Everyone is entitled in full equality to a fair and public hearing by an independent and impartial tribunal, in the determination of his rights and obligations and of any criminal charge against him.

Article 11. (1) Everyone charged with a penal offence has the right to be presumed innocent until proved guilty according to law in a public trial at which he has had all the guarantees necessary for his defence.
(2) No one shall be held guilty of any penal offence on account of any act or omission which did not constitute a penal offence, under national or international law, at the time when it was committed. Nor shall a heavier penalty be imposed than the one that was applicable at the time the penal offence was committed.

Article 12. No one shall be subjected to arbitrary interference with his privacy, family, home or correspondence, nor to attacks upon his honour and reputation. Everyone has the right to the protection of the law against such interference or attacks.

Article 13. (1) Everyone has the right to freedom of movement and residence within the borders of each state.
(2) Everyone has the right to leave any country, including his own, and to return to his country.

Article 14. (1) Everyone has the right to seek and to enjoy in other countries asylum from persecution.
(2) This right may not be invoked in the case of prosecutions genuinely arising from non-political crimes or from acts contrary to the purposes and principles of the United Nations.

Article 15. (1) Everyone has the right to a nationality.
(2) No one shall be arbitrarily deprived of his nationality nor denied the right to change his nationality.

Article 16. (1) Men and women of full age, without any limitation due to race, nationality or religion, have the right to marry and to found a family. They are entitled to equal rights as to marriage, during marriage and at its dissolution.
(2) Marriage shall be entered into only with the free and full consent of the intending spouses.
(3) The family is the natural and fundamental group unit of society and is entitled to protection by society and the State.

Article 17. (1) Everyone has the right to own property alone as well as in association with others.

(2) No one shall be arbitrarily deprived of his property.

Article 18. Everyone has the right to freedom of thought, conscience and religion; this right includes freedom to change his religion or belief, and freedom, either alone or in community with others and in public or private, to manifest his religion or belief in teaching, practice, worship and observance.

Article 19. Everyone has the right to freedom of opinion and expression; this right includes freedom to hold opinions without interference and to seek, receive and impart information and ideas through any media and regardless of frontiers.

Article 20. (1) Everyone has the right to freedom of peaceful assembly and association.

(2) No one may be compelled to belong to an association.

Article 21. (1) Everyone has the right to take part in the government of his country, directly or through freely chosen representatives.

(2) Everyone has the right of equal access to public service in his country.

(3) The will of the people shall be the basis of the authority of government; this will shall be expressed in periodic and genuine elections which shall be by universal and equal suffrage and shall be held by secret vote or by equivalent free voting procedures.

Article 22. Everyone, as a member of society, has the right to social security and is entitled to realization, through national effort and international cooperation and in accordance with the organization and resources of each State, of the economic, social and cultural rights indispensable for his dignity and the free development of his personality.

Article 23. (1) Everyone has the right to work, to free choice of employment, to just and favourable conditions of work and to protection against unemployment.

(2) Everyone, without any discrimination, has the right to equal pay for equal work.

(3) Everyone who works has the right to just and favourable remuneration ensuring for himself and his family an existence worthy of human dignity, and supplemented, if necessary, by other means of social protection.

(4) Everyone has the right to form and to join trade unions for the protection of his interests.

Article 24. Everyone has the right to rest and leisure, including reasonable limitation of working hours and periodic holidays with pay.

Article 25. (1) Everyone has the right to a standard of living adequate for the health and well-being of himself and of his family, including food, clothing, housing and medical care and necessary social services, and the right to security in the event of unemployment, sickness, disability, widowhood, old age or other lack of livelihood in circumstances beyond his control.

(2) Motherhood and childhood are entitled to special care and assistance. All children, whether born in or out of wedlock, shall enjoy the same social protection.

Article 26. (1) Everyone has the right to education. Education shall be free, at least in the elementary and fundamental stages. Elementary education shall be compulsory. Technical and professional education shall be made generally available and higher education shall be equally accessible to all on the basis of merit.

(2) Education shall be directed to the full development of the human personality and to the strengthening of respect for human rights and fundamental freedoms. It shall promote understanding, tolerance and friendship among all nations, racial or

religious groups, and shall further the activities of the United Nations for the maintenance of peace.

(3) Parents have a prior right to choose the kind of education that shall be given to their children.

Article 27. (1) Everyone has the right freely to participate in the cultural life of the community, to enjoy the arts and to share in scientific advancement and its benefits.

(2) Everyone has the right to the protection of the moral and material interests resulting from any scientific, literary or artistic production of which he is the author.

Article 28. Everyone is entitled to a social and international order in which the rights and freedoms set forth in this Declaration can be fully realized.

Article 29. (1) Everyone has duties to the community in which alone the free and full development of his personality is possible.

(2) In the exercise of his rights and freedoms, everyone shall be subject only to such limitations as are determined by law solely for the purpose of securing due recognition and respect for the rights and freedoms of others and of meeting the just requirements of morality, public order and the general welfare in a democratic society.

(3) These rights and freedoms may in no case be exercised contrary to the purposes and principles of the United Nations.

Article 30. Nothing in this Declaration may be interpreted as implying for any State, group or person any right to engage in any activity or to perform any act aimed at the destruction of any of the rights and freedoms set forth herein.

Appendix C
Principles for Ethical Practice
of Assertive Behavior Training

As AT gained in popularity during the mid-1970's, an increasing concern developed among responsible practitioners for the misuse of the process: unqualified trainers, illegitimate purposes, contraindicated clients. At the December 1975 meeting of the Association for Advancement of Behavior Therapy in San Francisco, a group of nationally recognized AT professionals met to initiate work on a statement of ethical principles. The following statement is the result of their work.

Further discussion of this proposal occurred at the First International Conference on Assertive Behavior Training in Washington, D.C., in August, 1976, and at the Association for Advancement of Behavior Therapy in New York City, December, 1976. Although no amendments to the original statement have been formalized, considerable concern has been expressed about the academic credentials suggested herein for qualifying facilitators. It is likely that a competency based criterion for qualification will emerge.

Moreover, AABT itself is preparing a statement of ethics for the practice of behavior therapy generally, which may have direct application to AT, although AT is not considered solely a "behavior therapy" by a considerable number of its practitioners.

Meanwhile, however, this statement remains the only public declaration by a group of professionals which is directed toward greater ethical responsibility in the practice of AT. Practitioners are urged to consider its implications for their own work.

With the increasing popularity of assertive behavior training, a quality of "faddishness" has become evident, and there are frequent reports of ethically irresponsible practices (and practitioners). We hear of trainers who, for example, do not adequately differentiate assertion and aggression. Others have failed to advocate proper ethical responsibility and caution to clients—e.g., failed to alert them to and/or prepare them for the possibility of retaliation or other highly negative reactions from others.

The following statement of "Principles for Ethical Practice of Assertive Behavior Training" is the work of the professional psychologists and educators listed below, who are actively engaged in the practice of facilitating assertive behavior (also referred to as "assertive therapy," "social skills training," "personal effectiveness training," and "AT"). We don't intend by this statement to discourage untrained individuals from becoming more assertive on their own, and we don't advocate that one must have extensive credentials in order to be of help to friends and relatives. Rather, these principles are offered to help foster responsible and ethical teaching and practice by human services professionals. Others who wish to enhance their own assertiveness or that of associates are encouraged to do so, with awareness of their own limitations, and of the importance of seeking help from a qualified therapist/trainer when necessary.

We hereby declare support for and adherence to the statement of principles, and invite responsible professionals in our own and other fields who use these techniques to join us in advocating and practicing these principles.

Robert E. Alberti, Ph.D.   Michael L. Emmons, Ph.D.
San Luis Obispo, CA   San Luis Obispo, CA

Iris G. Fodor, Ph.D.
Associate Professor, Educational Psychology
New York University, Washington Square
New York, NY

John Galassi, Ph.D.
School of Education
University of North Carolina
Chapel Hill, NC

Merna D. Galassi, Ed.D.
Meredith College
Raleigh, NC

Lynne Garnett, Ph.D.
Counseling Psychologist
University of California
Los Angeles, CA

Patricia Jakubowski, Ed.D.
Associate Professor, Behavioral Studies
University of Missouri
St. Louis, MO

Janet L. Wolfe, Ph.D.
Director of Clinical Services
Institute for Advanced Study in Rational
  Psychotherapy
New York, NY

1. Definition of Assertive Behavior

For purposes of these principles and the ethical framework expressed herein, we define assertive behavior as that complex of behaviors, emitted by a person in an interpersonal context, which express that person's feelings, attitudes, wishes, opinions or rights directly, firmly, and honestly, while respecting the feelings, attitudes, wishes, opinions and rights of the other person(s). Such behavior may include the expression of such emotions as anger, fear, caring, hope, joy, despair, indignation, embarrassment, but in any event is expressed in a manner which does not violate the rights of others. Assertive behavior is differentiated from aggressive behavior which, while expressive of one person's feelings, attitudes, wishes, opinions or rights, does not respect those characteristics in others.

While this definition is intended to be comprehensive, it is recognized that any adequate definition of assertive behavior must consider several dimensions:

A. *Intent:* behavior classified as assertive is not intended by its author to be hurtful of others.

B. *Behavior:* behavior classified as assertive would be evaluated by an "objective observer" as itself honest, direct, expressive and non-destructive of others.

C. *Effects:* behavior classified as assertive has the effect upon the receiver of a direct and non-destructive message, by which a "reasonable person" would not be hurt.

D. *Socio-cultural Context:* behavior classified as assertive is appropriate to the environment and culture in which it is exhibited, and may not be considered "assertive" in a different socio-cultural environment.

2. Client Self-Determination

These principles recognize and affirm the inherent dignity and the equal and inalienable rights of all members of the human family, as proclaimed in the "Universal Declaration of Human Rights" endorsed by the General Assembly of the United Nations.

Pursuant to the precepts of the Declaration, each client (trainee, patient) who seeks assertive behavior training shall be treated as a person of value, with all of the freedoms and rights expressed in the Declaration. No procedure shall be utilized in the name of assertive behavior training which would violate those freedoms or rights.

Informed client self-determination shall guide all such interventions:

A. the client shall be fully informed in advance of all procedures to be utilized;
B. the client shall have the freedom to choose to participate or not at any point in the intervention;
C. the client who is institutionalized shall be similarly treated with respect and without coercion, insofar as is possible within the institutional environment.
D. the client shall be provided with explicit definitions of assertiveness and assertive training.
E. the client shall be fully informed as to the education, training, experience or other qualifications of the assertive trainer(s).
F. the client shall be informed as to the goals and potential outcomes of assertive training, including potentially high levels of anxiety, and possible negative reactions from others.
G. the client shall be fully informed as to the responsibility of the assertion trainer(s) and the client(s).
H. the client shall be informed as to the ethics and employment of confidentiality guidelines as they pertain to various assertive training settings (e.g. clinical vs. non-clinical).

3. Qualifications of Facilitators

Assertive behavior training is essentially a therapeutic procedure, although frequently practiced in a variety of settings by professionals not otherwise engaged in rendering a "psychological" service. Persons in any professional role who engage in helping others to change their behavior, attitudes, and interpersonal relationships must understand human behavior at a level commensurate with the level of their interventions.

3.1 General Qualifications

We support the following minimum, general qualifications for facilitators at all levels of intervention (including "trainers in training"—preservice or inservice—who are preparing for professional service in a recognized human services field, and who may be conducting assertive behavior training under supervision as part of a research project or practicum):

A. Fundamental understanding of the principles of learning and behavior (equivalent to completion of a rigorous undergraduate level course in learning theory);
B. Fundamental understanding of anxiety and its effects upon behavior (equivalent to completion of a rigorous undergraduate level course in abnormal psychology);
C. Knowledge of the limitations, contraindications and potential dangers of assertive behavior training; familiarity with theory and research in the area.
D. Satisfactory evidence of competent performance as a facilitator, as observed by a qualified trainer, is strongly recommended for all professionals, particularly for those who do not possess a doctorate or an equivalent level of training. Such evidence would most ideally be supported by:
1) participation in at least ten (10) hours of assertive behavior training as a client (trainee, patient); and
2) participation in at least ten (10) hours of assertive behavior training as a facilitator under supervision.

3.2 Specific Qualifications

The following additional qualifications are considered to be the minimum expected for facilitators at the indicated levels of intervention:

A. *Assertive behavior training*, including non-clinical workshops, groups, and individual client training aimed at teaching assertive skills to those persons who require only encouragement and specific skill training, and in whom no serious emotional deficiency or pathology is evident.

1) For trainers in programs conducted under the sponsorship of a recognized human services agency, school, governmental or corporate entity, church, or community organization:

   a) An advanced degree in a recognized field of human services (e.g. psychology, counseling, social work, medicine, public health, nursing, education, human development, theology/divinity), including at least one term of field experience in a human services agency supervised by a qualified trainer; *or*

   b) certification as a minister, public school teacher, social worker, physician, counselor, nurse, or clinical, counseling, educational, or school psychologist, or similar human services professional, as recognized by the state wherein employed or by the recognized state or national professional society in the indicated discipline; *or*

   c) one year of paid counseling experience in a recognized human services agency, supervised by a qualified trainer; *or*

   d) qualification under items 3.2B or 3.2C below.

2) For trainers in programs including interventions at the level defined in this item (3.2A), but without agency/organization sponsorship:

   a) An advanced degree in a recognized field of human services (e.g. psychology, counseling, social work, medicine, public health, nursing, education, human development, theology/divinity) including at least one term of field experience in a human services agency supervised by a qualified trainer; *and*

   b) certification as a minister, social worker, physician, counselor, nurse, or clinical, counseling, educational, or school psychologist, or similar human services professional, as recognized by the state wherein employed or by the recognized state or national professional society in the indicated discipline; *or*

   c) qualification under items 3.2B or 3.2C below.

B. *Assertive behavior therapy*, including clinical interventions designed to assist persons who are severely inhibited by anxiety, or who are significantly deficient in social skills, or who are controlled by aggression, or who evidence pathology, or for whom other therapeutic procedures are indicated:

1) For therapists in programs conducted under the sponsorship of a recognized human services agency, school, governmental or corporate entity, church, or community organization:

   a) An advanced degree in a recognized field of human services (e.g. psychology, counseling, social work, medicine, public health, nursing, education, human development, theology/divinity) including at least one term of field experience in a human services agency supervised by a qualified trainer; *or*

   b) certification as a minister, social worker, physician, counselor, nurse, or clinical, counseling, educational, or school psychologist, as recognized by the state wherein employed or by the recognized state or national professional society in the indicated discipline; *or*

   c) qualification under item 3.2C below.

2) For therapists employing interventions at the level defined in this item (3.2B), but without agency/organization sponsorship:

   a) An advanced degree in a recognized field of human services (e.g. psychology, counseling, social work, medicine, public health, nursing, education, human development, theology/divinity) including at least one term of field experience in a human services agency supervised by a qualified trainer; *and*

b) certification as minister, social worker, physician, counselor, nurse, or clinical, counseling, educational, or school psychologist, as recognized by the state wherein employed or by the recognized state or national professional society in the indicated discipline; *and*

c) at least one year of paid professional experience in a recognized human services agency, supervised by a qualified trainer; *or*

d) qualification under item 3.2C below.

C. *Training of trainers*, including preparation of other professionals to offer assertive behavior training/therapy to clients, in school, agency, organization, or individual settings.

1) A doctoral degree in a recognized field of human services (e.g. psychology, counseling, social work, medicine, public health, nursing, education, human development, theology/divinity) including at least one term of field experience in a human services agency supervised by a qualified trainer; *and*

2) certification as a minister, social worker, physician, counselor, nurse, or clinical, counseling, educational, or school psychologist, as recognized by the state wherein employed, or by the recognized state or national professional society in the indicated discipline; *and*

3) at least one year of paid professional experience in a recognized human services agency, supervised by a qualified trainer; *and*

4) advanced study in assertive behavior training/therapy, including at least two of the following:

a) At least thirty (30) hours of facilitation with clients;

b) participation in at least two different workshops at professional meetings or professional training institutes:

c) contribution to the professional literature in the field.

3.3 We recognize that counselors and psychologists are not certified by each state. In states wherein no such certification is provided, unless contrary to local statute, we acknowledge the legitimacy of professionals who: A) are otherwise qualified under the provisions of items 3.1 and 3.2; and B) would be eligible for certification as a counselor or psychologist in another state.

3.4 We do not consider that participation in one or two workshops on assertive behavior, even though conducted by a professional with an advanced degree, is adequate qualification to offer assertive behavior training to others, *unless the additional qualifications* of items 3.1 and 3.2 are also met.

3.5 These qualifications are presented as *standards* for professional facilitators of assertive behavior. No ''certification'' or ''qualifying'' agency is hereby proposed. Rather, it is incumbent upon each professional to evaluate himself/herself as a trainer/therapist according to these standards, and to make explicit to clients the adequacy of his/her qualifications as a facilitator.

4. Ethical Behavior of Facilitators

Since the encouragement and facilitation of assertive behavior is essentially a *therapeutic* procedure, the ethical standards most applicable to the practice of assertive behavior training are those of psychologists. We recognize that many persons who practice some form of assertive behavior training are not otherwise engaged in rendering a "psychological" service (i.e. teachers, personnel/training directors). To all we support the statement of "Ethical Standards for Psychologists" as adopted by the American Psychological Association as the standard of ethical behavior by which assertive behavior training shall be conducted.

We recognize that the methodology employed in assertive behavior training may include a wide range of procedures, some of which are of unproven value. It is the responsibility of the facilitators to inform clients of any experimental procedures. Under no circumstances should the facilitator "guarantee" a specific outcome from an intervention.

5. Appropriateness of Assertive Behavior Training Interventions

Assertive behavior training, as any intervention oriented toward helping people change, may be applied under a wide range of conditions, yet its appropriateness must be evaluated in each individual case. The responsible selection of assertive behavior training for a particular intervention must include attention to at least the following dimensions:

A. *Client ·* The personal characteristics of the client in question (age, sex, ethnicity, institutionalization, capacity for informed choice, physical and psychological functionality).

B. *Problem/Goals:* The purpose for which professional help has been sought or recommended (job skills, severe inhibition, anxiety reduction, overcome aggression).

C. *Facilitator:* The personal and professional qualifications of the facilitator in question (age, sex, ethnicity, skills, understanding, ethics—see also Principles 3 and 4 above).

D. *Setting:* The characteristics of the setting in which the intervention is conducted (home, school, business, agency, clinic, hospital, prison). Is the client free to choose? Is the facilitator's effectiveness systematically evaluated?

E. *Time/Duration:* The duration of the intervention. Does the time involved represent a brief word of encouragement, a formal training workshop, an intensive and long-term therapeutic effort?

F. *Method:* The nature of the intervention. Is it "packaged" procedure or tailored to client needs? Is training based on sound principles of learning and behavior? Is there clear differentiation of aggressiveness, assertiveness and other concepts? Are definitions, techniques, procedures and purposes clarified? Is care taken to encourage small, successful steps and to minimize punishing consequences? Are any suggested "homework assignments" presented with adequate supervision, responsibility, and sensitivity to the effect upon significant others of the client's behavior change efforts? Are clients informed that assertiveness "doesn't always work?"

G. *Outcome:* Are there follow-up procedures, either by self-report or other post-test procedures?

6. Social Responsibility

Assertive behavior training shall be conducted within the law. Trainers and clients are encouraged to work assertively to change those laws which they consider need to be changed, and to modify the social system in ways they believe appropriate—in particular to extend the boundaries of human rights. Toward these ends, trainers are encouraged to facilitate responsible change skills via assertive behavior training. All those who practice, teach, or do research on assertive behavior are urged to advocate caution and ethical responsibility in application of the technique, in accordance with these Principles.

Bibliography

Alberti, R.E. & Emmons, M.L. *Your Perfect Right: A Guide to Assertive Behavior*. San Luis Obispo, California: Impact Publishers, Inc., 1970, 1974, 1978, 1982.

Augsberger, D. *Anger and Assertiveness in Pastoral Care*. Philadelphia: Fortress Press, 1979.

Bach, G. and Wyden, P. *The Intimate Enemy: How to Fight Fair in Love and Marriage*. New York: William Morrow, 1968.

Baer, J. *How to Be an Assertive [not Aggressive] Woman in Life, in Love, and on the Job*. New York: Signet (New American Library), 1976.

Beck, A. *Cognitive Therapy and the Emotional Disorders*. New York: New American Library, 1979.

Bloom, L.Z., Coburn, K. and Pearlman, J. *The New Assertive Woman*. New York: Delacorte Press, 1975.

Bolles, R.N. *What Color Is Your Parachute?* Berkeley,California: Ten Speed Press, 1986 (annual).

Bower, S.A. & Bower, G.H. *Asserting Yourself.* Reading: MA: Addison-Wesley, 1976.

Buscaglia, L. *Love*. New York: Fawcett, 1981.

Cheek, D.K. *Assertive Black...Puzzled White*. San Luis Obispo, California: Author, 1976.

Cooley, M.L. and Hollandsworth, J.G., A strategy for teaching verbal content of assertive responses. In R.E. Alberti (ed.) *Assertiveness: Innovations, Applications, Issues*. San Luis Obispo, California: Impact Publishers, 1977 (now out of print, but available in many libraries).

Cotler, S.B. and Guerra, J.J. *Assertion Training: A Humanistic-Behavioral Guide to Self-Dignity*. Champaign, Illinois, Research Press, 1976.

Davis, M., Eshelman, E., McKay, M. *The Relaxation and Stress Reduction Workbook*. Richmond, California: New Harbinger Publications, 1980.

Ellis, A. & Harper, R. *A New Guide to Rational Living*. Hollywood, California: Wilshire Books, 1979.

Emery, G. *Own Your Own Life*. New York: Signet, 1984.

Emmons, M.L. *The Inner Source: A Guide to Meditative Therapy*. San Luis Obispo, California: Author, 1978.

Emmons, M. & Richardson, D. *The Assertive Christian*. Minneapolis: Winston Press, 1981.

Fensterheim, H. and Baer, J. *Don't Say Yes When You Want to Say No*. New York: Dell, 1975.

Fromm, E. *The Art of Loving*. New York: Harper and Row, 1956.

Gordon, T. *Parent Effectiveness Training*. New York: Wyden, 1970.

Griffin-Lawson, L., Donant, F.D., and Lawson, J.D. *Lead On!*. San Luis Obispo, California: Impact Publishers, 1976.

Haney, M. & Boenisch, E. *StressMap*. San Luis Obispo, California: Impact Publishers, Inc., 1982.

Hastings, A., Fadiman, J., Gordon, J. *Health for the Whole Person*. Boulder, Colorado: Westview Press, 1980.

Hunt, Morton, The lessons of the cliff. *Parade Magazine*, July 14, 1985.

Lange, A.J. and Jakubowski, P. *The Assertive Option*. Champaign, Illinois: Research Press, 1978.

Lazarus, A.A. *Marital Myths*. San Luis Obispo, California: Impact Publishers, 1985.

Lazarus, A.A., and Fay A. *I Can If I Want To*. New York: William Morrow, 1975.

Palmer, P. *Liking Myself*. San Luis Obispo, California: Impact Publishers, Inc., 1977.

Palmer, P. *The Mouse, the Monster, and Me: Assertiveness for Young People*. San Luis Obispo, California: Impact Publishers, Inc., 1977.

Pelletier, K. *Holistic Medicine*. New York: Delacorte Press/ Seymour Lawrence, 1979.

Phelps, S. and Austin, N. *The Assertive Woman*. San Luis Obispo, California: Impact Publishers, Inc., 1975.

Rathus, S.A. *BT: Behavior Therapy*. New York: Doubleday, 1978.

Rogers, C.R. *On Becoming a Person*. Boston: Houghton-Mifflin, 1961.

Salter, A. *Conditioned Reflex Therapy*. New York: Farrar, Straus, and Giroux, 1949 (Capricorn Books edition, 1961).

Seligman, M.E. Fall into helplessness. *Psychology Today*, 1973, June, 43.

Serber, M. Book review of *Your Perfect Right*, *Behavior Therapy* 1971, *2*, 253-354.

Sheehy, G. *Passages: Predictable Crises of Adult Life*. New York: E.P. Dutton and Company, 1976.

Simon, S.B. *Values Clarification*. New York: Hart Publishing Co., 1972.

Tanabe-Endsley, P. *Project Write*. El Cerrito, California: Author, 1974, 1979. (1421 Arlington, 94530)

Tavris, C. *Anger: The Misunderstood Emotion*. New York: Simon and Schuster, 1982.

Time Magazine. Is the revolution over? New York: Author, April 19, 1984

Ulene, A. *Feeling Fine*. New York: St. Martin's Press, 1977.

Wolfe, J. and Fodor, I.G. A cognitive-behavioral approach to modifying assertive behavior in women. *The Counseling Psychologist*, 1975, *5*, 45-52.

Wolpe, J. *The Practice of Behavior Therapy*. New York: Pergamon Press, 1973 (2nd edition).

Index

Aggressive behavior, 11, 27, 29, 30, 31, 32, 35, 42, 98, 102, 141, 161, 184, 201
Alberti, L.B., 145
Alda, A., 5, 69
Anger, 125-138
Anxiety, 85-92
Appendices, 193-213
Assertive behavior, 3, 7, 8, 12, 13, 14, 19, 26, 31, 34, 43, 44, 45, 51, 68, 69, 72, 95, 97, 98, 122, 130, 142, 179, 187, 190, 201, 206
Assertive behavior, definition, 7, 26
Assertiveness inventory, 56-57
Attitudes, 73-83
Austin, N., 9, 10, 141

Beck, A., 51
Behavior change, 75, 137, 177
Behavior shaping, 104
Behavior therapy, 52, 91, 95, 96, 109
Behavioral Model for Personal Growth, 66-67
Body language, 161, 164
Body posture, 19, 45, 102
Boenisch, E., 91
Bolles, R.N., 146
Breathing, 86, 87

Cheek, D., 53
Children, 2, 9, 10, 11, 13, 38, 39, 40, 42, 55, 71, 118-122, 142, 154, 190, 195, 200, 201
Choice, 20, 21, 28, 72, 104, 127, 149, 164, 179-181, 199
Cognitive restructuring, 147
Competence, 155
Compliments, 113, 115, 176
Conflict resolution, 136, 137
Conflicts, 27, 143, 183
Consequences, 19, 28, 30, 33, 60, 67, 70, 81-82, 102, 130, 134, 179-182, 190
Consumer situations, 195-196
Content, 34, 52, 53, 54, 102, 126
Conversations, 26, 126
Cooley, M., 53
Criticism, 26, 39, 41, 88, 150-151, 197

Davis, M., 71
Decision-making, 14, 152
Desensitization, 90, 91
Diet, 132
Distance, 34, 46, 47, 173, 196
Divorce, 81, 126
DuBois, W.E.B., 101

Einstein, A., 95
Ellis, A., 51, 81
Emery, G., 81
Empathy, 166, 187
Eshelman, E.R., 71
Expression of feelings, 30, 121
Eye contact, 19, 20, 34, 45, 50-52, 68, 71, 102, 112, 149, 173, 177

Fears, 68, 85, 86, 87, 88, 91
Feedback, 15, 48, 50, 75, 97, 104, 120, 122, 142, 147, 151, 175, 182, 190
Fluency, 34, 49
Fodor, I., 121, 207
Forsberg, R., 69
Friendship, 26, 66, 116, 117, 118
Fromm, E., 110
Fuller, R.B., 109

Galassi, J., 207
Galassi, M., 207
Garnett, L., 207
Gestures, 34, 47, 50, 52, 68, 102, 142, 173
Ghandi, M.K., 190
Goals, 3, 8, 12, 17, 20, 21, 23, 26, 27-30, 33, 54, 60-61, 63-72, 74, 81, 82, 93, 98-101, 104, 107, 109, 118, 122, 127, 133, 136, 138, 154, 175
Guilt, 12, 30, 41, 121, 122

Haney, M., 91
Harper, R., 81
Hayes, W., 28
Holistic health, 185
Hollandsworth, J., 53
Holmes, O.W., 191
Honesty, 10, 12, 43, 54, 69, 75, 119, 152, 160
Human rights, 8, 83, 119, 120, 202

Indirect aggression, 30, 141, 161
Intimacy, 10, 12, 47, 159, 161, 167, 169

Jakubowski, P., 207
James, W., 157
Job, assertiveness on the, 145-155
Job interviews, 103, 154, 177
Johnson, S., 69
Juarez, B., 35

King, M.L., Jr., 190

Lazarus, A.A., 158
Listening, 34, 50, 51, 66, 71, 148, 167
Listening skills, 51, 167
Longfellow, H.W., 139

Making a request, 53, 143
Management, 9, 134, 138, 152
Marriage, 27, 112, 125, 141, 167
McKay, M., 71
Meichenbaum, D., 51, 77
Modeling, 68-69

Negotiation, 131, 137, 161
Neruda, P., 171
Niebuhr, R., 179
Nin, A., 73
Nonassertive behavior, 30, 31
Nonverbal behavior, 43-54

Palmer, P., 121
Parents and children, 118
Persistence, 69, 187, 188
Phelps, S., 9, 10, 141
Phobias, 88
Positive thoughts, 80, 103
Posture, 19, 34, 44, 45, 46, 52, 102, 173
Powerlessness, 5
Put-downs, 26, 139, 140, 141, 142, 143, 144

Rathus, S., 91
Rehearsal, behavior, 101-105
Relaxation, 64, 66, 71, 87, 90, 133, 138, 147
Relaxation exercises, 90
Risks, 74, 85, 117, 166, 183
Rogers, C.R., 65, 66

Salter, A., 55
Self-affirmation, 26
Self-concept, 31, 77
Self-confidence, 5, 47, 69, 80, 185
Self-control, 28, 185
Self-defeating behavior, 14, 97
Self-esteem, 27
Self-evaluation, 97
Self-help, 91, 92, 165
Self-respect, 137
Self-statements, 77, 79, 80, 82, 96
Self-worth, 2, 30, 75, 97
Serber, M., 45, 49, 109
Sexual behavior, 27
Sexual Communication Types, 162-163
Sexuality, 27, 157, 158, 161, 166, 167, 199
Sheehy, G., 12
Shyness, 160
SUD scale, 86, 87
Supervising, 151
Systematic desensitization, 90

Tanabe-Endsley, P., 87
Tavris, C., 130
Tension, 66, 86, 132
Thoreau, H.D., 43, 190
Thought stopping, 78, 79, 80, 82
Thoughts, 18, 51, 52, 73, 76, 77, 79, 80, 81, 82, 95, 97, 102, 103, 105, 144, 161, 163, 191
Tutu, D., 190

Universal Declaration of Human Rights, 202-205

Verbal behavior, 161, 173
Voice tone, 48, 177
Voice volume, 68

Walesa, L., 190
Wilder, T., 188
Wolfe, J., 121, 207
Wolpe, J., 25, 79, 90